Education
of a
Traveler

Adventures in Learning Around the Globe

BILL YEARGIN

IGNITE
PRESS
Fresno, CA

Published in the United States by
Ignite Press
5070 N 6th St. #189
Fresno, CA 93710
www.IgnitePress.us

ISBN: 978-1-953655-41-7 (Amazon Print)
ISBN: 978-1-953655-42-4 (IngramSpark) PAPERBACK
ISBN: 978-1-953655-43-1 (IngramSpark) HARDCOVER
ISBN: 978-1-953655-44-8 (E-book)

Library of Congress Control Number: 2020925852

Cover design by Ryan Lause
Edited by Samantha Maxwell
Interior design by Jetlaunch Layout Services

OTHER BOOKS BY BILL YEARGIN

Yeargin on Management
What Would Dad Say? Now That He's in Heaven
Making Life Better: The Correct Craft Story
Education of a CEO

To my family, who have not only tolerated but also joined my adventures.

Acknowledgements

To my cousin, thought partner, and editor Alex Gurtis. And to both Stephanie Clarke and Leigh. Your comments were all appreciated and made this book much better.

Table of Contents

Preface

110 countries? Yep.

Who does that? Apparently, me.

Did you see it coming? Nope.

Life is an incredible trip that occasionally takes us where we don't expect, with adventures we never could have imagined that sometimes scare us and other times delight. Whether those places are fun or frightening, we always, *always*, learn something that becomes an integral part of our education.

As a not particularly stellar student (A's and B's) trying to learn accounting at Palm Beach Community College, my aspirations were not much different than that of my peers: Marry a pretty girl (I hit a home run there), get a job at a "Big Eight" accounting firm (despite a horrible interview, did that), pass the CPA exam (yep, and it was brutal), and someday become a partner in the "Big Eight" accounting firm (nope, let that goal go when I realized accounting wasn't for me). I had not voyaged much farther away from my Florida home than North Carolina, and I didn't consider global travel much of a possibility—and, if I *did* think about global travel, it seemed scary.

A strange knack for being in the right place at the right time (most people call it luck) combined with an ever-growing passion for learning and experiencing new things changed that, however, and resulted in me spending the next forty years traveling the globe and visiting over 110 countries. I have had a lifetime of "once-in-a-lifetime" experiences.

It all began when my wife, Leigh, started a job at Eastern Airlines. We were able to fly pretty much anywhere in the world for very little—almost free—and would sometimes go to the airport on a Friday night with no idea where we were going for the weekend. We'd just get on flights that had empty seats. More than once, we ended up in a cold place when we had packed clothes for warm weather or popped in on distant relatives with little notice.

Our first transatlantic trip was to London, and Leigh was upgraded to first class while I sat back in coach. I was in the middle seat for the overnight flight, cramped between two people larger than their seats and could not sleep at all when I decided to check on Leigh. That was a mistake. Leigh was sound asleep on a lay flat seat with a nice blanket and pillow ensuring she was comfortable. And, to top it off, there was a half-eaten shrimp cocktail on her food tray.

Still, despite having not been a traveler, those first trips were exhilarating and inspired me to create a goal—which I quickly reached—of visiting all fifty U.S. states. At the time, visiting every state seemed like the ultimate travel experience.

A few years later, I became a popular speaker for boating industry events, a job that took me to Europe, Asia, South America, and Australia. Many of those trips were taken with one or the other of my daughters as they got old enough to travel with me and, as homeschoolers, had the flexibility to come along.

Later, family travel, work travel, service trips, and just plain curiosity took me to the world's richest and poorest communities, the world's most beautiful and historic sites, and meetings with many powerful people, including seven invitations to the White House and an Oval Office meeting with President Obama.

Years of both travel and being an insatiable reader have materially impacted both my thinking and faith. In the pages that follow, I will share fun, exciting, and scary stories that have served as a unique traveler's education. I hope to help readers expand the way they see the world by sharing a front row seat to how I've been impacted by both global travel and being a reader. In turn, I hope my experiences and traveler's education encourages others to travel, keep learning, and maybe even expand their thinking a little too.

There's no greater adventure than embracing life as a learner.

Chapter 1

Learning vs. Knowing

The scientists, researchers, scholars all say it's true... But my buddies from high school say it isn't... It's so hard to know who to believe. —Popular social media post

You can be 100 percent wrong and feel 100 percent right.

The more right I feel, the more likely I am wrong.

Interacting with people all over the world makes one thing clear: Very few people actually seek truth. Yep, very few. Even the most critical thinkers I know only seem to seek truth in areas where they have no strong opinion. Otherwise, they do what most everyone else does: They seek information that will support what they already believe. Most people don't want truth, they want validation.

They are not learners, they are knowers.

Much to the surprise of many fellow Americans, some of my favorite travels have been throughout the Middle East. Whether in Israel, Jordan, Egypt, Dubai, Abu Dhabi, Bahrain, Qatar, Saudi Arabia, or Kuwait, I have been treated well and felt safe. Some people seriously doubt my experience or sanity (okay, maybe they have some basis for questioning my sanity, but not for this) when I tell them about my Middle East experiences. This is especially true in a post-9/11 environment where the Middle East seems like a scary place to most Americans.

They have a hard time believing that while my trips there have been adventurous and I have had experiences that pushed me outside my comfort zone, the people always treated me well with a glaring exception I will share later. There is no amount of sharing my experiences that can change what they "know" about the Middle East, even though they have never been there. Most people seem to prefer "knowing" over learning.

Irrational Thinking

As one way of feeding an insatiable desire to learn, I have taken several classes at Harvard over the years, and one of my favorite courses was Behavioral Economics, which is basically where psychology meets economics. I took the course after reading several fascinating books on the subject. There are lots of concepts and theories that essentially demonstrate that our thinking is not rational—we *think* we're rational, of course, but most of us aren't as rational as we think. One of the fundamental concepts of Behavioral Economics is an idea called confirmation bias, which causes us to understand information through a lens that confirms what we already believe (like thinking your sports team has a chance for a championship this year when any sane person would look at the data and know they will be cellar dwellers).

An interesting example of this was the recent COVID-19 pandemic. All the data released, no matter what it said, was manipulated in the minds of the people who consumed it to support the position they already held on the virus. There was little search for truth. The exact same data was used to prove that President Trump was the best president ever or the worst president ever or prove the entire experience was either fake news or being underreported or show how we should all be staying home in hermetically sealed dwellings or going to the movies together. People were not seeking truth— they were using data to validate what they thought they knew.

There is tremendous discomfort, but also power, in seeking truth. I am often asked by people younger than me (which, frankly, is getting to be most people) for advice, and I always give them the same counsel: Don't be a knower, be a learner.

Looking Through a Different Lens

Most Americans who grew up in the 1970s would likely feel a little strange visiting Ho Chi Minh City (formerly Saigon) in Vietnam, and I was no different.

I remember as a kid hearing the daily death count of Americans each night on the 6:30 p.m. news. Even more impactful was the concern that my family shared over my Uncle Neil, who was serving in the Air Force and stationed in Vietnam during the worst of the war. I remember the worry my father and grandmother shared, particularly one time when he was in the field for several days without the ability to contact anyone. It was a scary time, especially for those actually in "Viet Nam," as described by former Reagan administration Naval Secretary, James Webb, in his excellent novel, *Fields of Fire*. Even as a kid, the Vietnam era left an indelible mark on me.

Landing at Tan Son Nhat International Airport felt different than the first touchdown in most other countries. It felt almost forbidden, or even disloyal, to be there, but I was on a business trip in Asia and had a meeting there the next day. Honestly, though, my most prevalent feeling was excitement.

Taking a taxi from the airport was different in Ho Chi Minh City because we were one of the few cars on the road. Instead, there were millions of scooters.

Scooters swarm Ho Chi Minh City, and much of the city has roundabouts that don't require them to stop. This makes getting across the street interesting because it is impossible to cross in the traditional Western sense: Wait for the light to change, look for the green sign, and walk across comfortably. Nope! In fact, crossing in Ho Chi Minh City was much more akin to a suicide trek. The first time I crossed a street, I stood on the curb for a long time and honestly did not know how I would get across. The innumerable scooters kept passing by, and the locals I watched cross the street seemed to have some type of invisible protection shield I could not see because I had no idea how they were doing it. Finally, a kind lady asked if she could help me get across—think the reverse of the boy scout story. After some cajoling, I took her advice and just stepped off the curb and walked across. Fortunately, she was right, and the scooter drivers didn't want to hit me any more than I wanted to be hit, so they just scooted by as I nervously played human Frogger.

My meeting in Vietnam was cancelled, so I ended up with a few hours to check out Ho Chi Minh City and took in several of the tourist sites, including Reunification Palace and the War Remnants Museum. In the War Remnants Museum, I was able to see the Vietnam War through a different set of eyes. The museum presented American atrocities that are well-documented in the U.S. but not discussed much. Rather than just dismiss the Vietnamese perspective shared by the museum, I wanted to understand how they viewed the war and the U.S. participation, which, not surprisingly, is much different than the perspective most Americans have. I wanted to be a "Learner." I did not want to be a "Knower" who either dismisses, won't even listen to, or listens so biasedly to other perspectives that they lose an incredible opportunity to grow.

Kathryn Schultz in her wonderful book *Being Wrong* explains why different people can see the same exact thing but interpret it in completely different ways. Learners try to understand, appreciate, and value the differences, while knowers look for data to support their predetermined position. Knowers try to shift reality to fit their perspectives, dismissing those differences entirely.

French novelist Marcel Proust said that much more important than seeing new lands is seeing old lands with new eyes. That's the approach of a Learner.

Presidential Learning

Meeting a President is always fun, especially if they are in office. Years ago, I was able to meet Ronald Reagan when he visited my college. Waiting for him with his Secret Service detail and eventually shaking his hand was thrilling. He took the time to look me in the eye and make me feel important, which was a gift I will never forget. Meeting Jimmy Carter, Bill Clinton, and George W. Bush after they left office was an honor, but being invited to the White House to meet President Obama and, later, President Trump while they were the sitting Presidents was an experience unlike few others. Being in the Oval Office and thinking about the history of that room and the decisions that were made there made me feel small (in a good way) and humbled.

Fast forward to 2017. I was enjoying a University of Central Florida football game with Leigh when I received a call from Washington, D.C. I normally don't answer calls if I don't have the caller in my contacts, but I decided to take this one. The caller identified herself as a member of Vice President Pence's staff who said she was at my office to determine if our Orlando factory would be a good site for a visit by the Vice President. Leigh and I left the game and drove to my office where they were waiting outside the gate because our security guard, Susie (all 90 pounds of her), would not let them on the property. She held her own against several cars that made up the Vice President's staff and secret service detail who were checking us out. Good for you, Susie!

It was the first time we had hosted a visit by the President or Vice President, and I had no idea what went into it, but boy, was I about to learn. After agreeing we would host the Vice President, we had four days to prepare. During those four days, we had a couple dozen of the Vice President's staff and security detail with us constantly. The whole event almost blew up (can I say it that way?) the night before Pence arrived when a background check on me turned up some articles I had written that, while not critical of the Administration, did not really align with their thinking. However, after a call with his Chief of Staff in Washington, D.C., during which I repeatedly assured them I would not embarrass the Vice President, the visit was confirmed.

When Pence arrived, the secret service drove his car into our building because they thought it would be more secure. I was honored to greet the Vice President and give him, Florida's then-Governor Rick Scott, and Secretary of Agriculture Sonny Perdue a tour of our Orlando plant. The tour itself was private, but after it, we had a roundtable event with the Vice President, and many of our employees were able to meet him. I was thrilled to have my mom and brother come up from West Palm Beach for the event, and someone took a candid picture I will always cherish of Mom talking to Vice President Pence and Governor Rick Scott, with them both listening to her carefully.

I never met Abraham Lincoln, but years ago, I visited his boyhood home. As a young boy, he grew up extremely poor in a Midwestern community. Lincoln's tough life was made harder when, at nine years old, his mother died and his father deserted both him and his sister. For months, Lincoln lived as a feral kid until his father eventually came back with a new wife.

Fortunately for Lincoln, his stepmother encouraged him to be a learner, and it changed the course of our country. Over and over, Lincoln demonstrated that he was the quintessential learner, even in the toughest of times. As Doris Kearns Goodwin writes in her great book *Team of Rivals*, Lincoln took this learner mentality with him into the White House by inviting his bitterest rivals to serve on his cabinet (sorta like Trump inviting Hillary Clinton to work with him). There is little chance that Abraham Lincoln, a dirt-poor boy from the Midwest with a challenging life, would have been able to serve our country when he was most needed without being a learner.

Choose to Be Happy

On a trip to Prague in the Czech Republic, my youngest daughter Amanda and I decided to travel about thirty miles north of town to visit the Terezin Concentration Camp used by the Nazis in WWII. While it wasn't a camp on the scale of Auschwitz or Treblinka, at least 30,000 Jews died at the facility. The visit reminded me of the book written by Victor Frankl, *Man's Search for Meaning*.

In *Man's Search for Meaning*, Frankl describes his time in four different concentration camps as a Jewish prisoner. While his wife and parents were killed at one of the camps, he was fortunate to survive a brutal few years. Frankl wrote his classic book shortly after the war and drew an impactful conclusion: People can take everything else away from us, but they can't take our ability to choose how we react.

I don't want to play psychologist, but I have seen over and over the impact our choices regarding how we want to view the world have on our mindset. Actually, real psychologist Lori Gottlieb, who wrote the interesting book *Maybe You Should Talk to Someone*, has stated that happiness is just math. In short, it is "your reality minus your expectations." I don't want to judge anyone, and I know that people have real struggles, but it seems that often, our happiness is highly dependent on how we choose to view our circumstances. We can learn to make the right choices.

Alone, Not Tandem

My CIA agent friend Michele says that nothing impactful happens in our comfort zone. I learned that firsthand by skydiving.

Before leaping out of a plane, I did my research and learned that only one of 200,000 skydiving jumps end in death (still a bad deal for that jumper). I also learned that skydiving is three times safer than driving, and based on my experience living in Orlando, that is probably true. However, despite the seemingly good odds, jumping out of an airplane still pushed me way out of my comfort zone.

Though it was clearly outside my comfort zone, I decided that I was going to do it. However, I didn't want to jump tandem as most first-time skydivers do—I wanted to jump out and skydive by myself. And, in hindsight, maybe that line of thinking is why the one of 200,000 die.

So, I took a day off work and drove out to Clewiston, Florida. After rejecting the recommendations from the staff at the skydive concession that I should tandem jump first (I was concerned I would only do it once and wanted to go all-in), I began the eight-hour Accelerated Freefall course. After finishing the course, we packed my parachute and took off in a plane so rickety I actually believed my odds were much better jumping out than trusting the plane to get me back to the ground. We climbed to a little over 12,000 feet, and after hanging half-in and half-out of the plane (literally) for what seemed like an eternity, I jumped.

Though I jumped by myself, I had two other jumpers with me, my instructor and a cameraman. The instructor saved my life.

In the Accelerated Freefall class, I learned that after jumping, I would be falling at 130 miles per hour and it was important that I check my altimeter every few seconds so I could be sure to pull my ripcord at 5,000 feet altitude. Then, after pulling the ripcord, my rate of falling would drop meaningfully and allow me a leisurely ride down to the X on which I was supposed to land.

Well, apparently, I went into sensory overload (seems likely given I was falling for the first time at 130 mph) and forgot to check my altimeter. If my instructor (who was doing all kinds of flips and other crazy stuff that partially distracted me—I'll use that as an excuse) had not come over and tapped on my altimeter at 4,500 feet, letting me know I needed to pull the ripcord, I would have fallen right into the earth.

Thankfully, he did point out my obvious and life-threatening mistake, and since you are reading this book, you know I survived. In fact, I had a perfect landing after circling and touching down right on the X.

Skydiving was fun, but the biggest lesson for me was that getting outside my comfort zone dramatically expanded my thinking. For a long time after my jump, everything seemed easier. It proved to me that the only way to expand our comfort zone is to get out of it — and, once we expand it, everything gets easier.

If there is one thing I have learned over the years, it is that life is more comfortable as a Knower but much more exciting as a Learner! We'll talk about this a bit more in the next chapters, where I explore my favorite travels and how rejecting "knowing" in favor of learning had a lasting impact upon me.

Reflections

- We can be 100 percent wrong and feel 100 percent right.
- I don't want to go through life as a "Knower."
- Life is much better as a "Learner."
- How we choose to view the world materially impacts our happiness and effectiveness.
- We dramatically grow when we deliberately get out of our comfort zone.

Chapter 2

Favorites

Whenever someone learns I have visited over 110 countries, they generally have three questions, usually in this order:

1. Where is your favorite place?
2. Where is the best food?
3. What places are still on your bucket list?

So, let's tackle the three questions before we get deeper in the book.

Question One: Places

I often answer the first question by explaining that, generally, the more different a destination is from where I live in the States—Florida—the better. I enjoy different sites, smells, foods, and people who not only look different than me but who also see the world differently. I enjoy being outside my comfort zone.

More specifically, the question is best answered by considering specific types of locales. For instance, there are different answers for my favorite city, a beach vacation, a historical location, etc. Even with that additional context, for some reason, it is hard for me to answer.

For cities, near the top of the list of my favorite places would be New York City, Sydney, Tokyo, Beijing, Bangkok, London, Paris, Budapest, Monaco, Rome, Casablanca, Athens, Dubai, Auckland, Hong Kong, and Havana. While my daughters were growing up, we went to New York City for a long weekend almost every year.

However, the city I was the most pleasantly surprised with was Budapest, Hungary, which is an amazing and underrated city—the Paris of Eastern Europe.

Amazing beach vacation spots would include Tahiti, The Maldives, The Seychelles, Bermuda (which is Leigh's favorite place), and much of the Caribbean but particularly St. Kitts. The Maldives were particularly interesting because it is a conservative Muslim country that is known for their spectacular beach resorts, which makes for an interesting combination.

Personally, for me, top historical spots were London, Paris, Beijing, Kyoto, Hiroshima, Vienna, Vatican City, Belfast, Vietnam, Havana, Agra, and Israel. I clearly remember my first trip to London and realizing they had pubs that were older than the United States. Israel is amazing because of the world and Biblical history that unfolded there.

In the U.S., it's hard to pick favorite spots because the whole country is so amazing, but if I had to, I would say Hawaii, Alaska, Yosemite, Grand Canyon, Yellowstone, The Badlands, Rocky Mountains, the coast of Maine, and the Florida Keys.

The above lists clearly don't do justice to all the things there are to experience in the world, but hopefully, it gives those readers who are aspiring travelers a good selection from which to start.

Question Two: Food

The best meals I have enjoyed travelling were undoubtedly at my grandmother's house in Oxford, North Carolina. She would make fried chicken that can't be duplicated, country ham, vegetables straight from my grandfather's garden, and homemade biscuits. Then she would top it off with homemade chocolate pie. I would be a rich man if I could replicate those meals and set up a restaurant selling them. A close second to Grandma's food was just down the street from her house in Henderson, North Carolina, at Nunnery Freeman BBQ. Unfortunately, Grandma passed away years ago and Nunnery's, as we called it, is closed, but I would pay a lot to duplicate either of those meals.

After Grandma's cooking and Nunnery's, probably the best meal I have enjoyed travelling was a lunch in the Golan Heights, just northeast of the Sea of Galilee. It was an amazing mixed grill that several people shared, and it was wonderfully delicious. Mixed grill must be popular in the Middle East because a close second to the Golan Heights lunch was a similar meal sitting on the shore of the Nile river in Cairo. I can't actually remember having a meal in the Middle East that was not delicious—it's a great destination for foodies.

I also remember one dinner on the top floor of my host's home in a Rio de Janeiro, Brazil, high-rise. The condominium opened on both sides for a total al fresco vibe. On one side of the condominium was Sugarloaf Mountain, and on the other was the iconic Christ the Redeemer statue. I cannot imagine there was a better view in all of Rio, maybe even in all of South America—and the dinner was as good as the view. Churrasco, the Brazilian BBQ mixed grill, was very tasty, although I am sure the remarkable view didn't hurt the flavor. We also enjoyed feijoada, which is a bean stew with beef that is probably Brazil's most famous dish.

While that night in Rio may have been my favorite South American meal, my experience is that food all across the continent is outstanding.

Question Three: Bucket List

Where I would still like to visit is a tough question because I am generally pretty content and know I have already been incredibly fortunate to see so much. I hate to be greedy! With that said, there are three places I would still enjoy visiting.

At the top of my bucket list is Antarctica. I had not really thought much about Antarctica until enjoying some coffee with then-Florida Governor Rick Scott in an Orlando Starbucks and hearing him share how much his family enjoyed going there. It was discouraging when I checked into it and realized the cruise ship that takes groups to Antarctica must pass through Drake's Passage, an experience often called the "Drake Shake." It is extremely rough. However, I recently learned there are planes that will shuttle people over Drake Shake and meet the cruise ship on the other side. That sounds like a plan to me.

I have been to Africa several times (more on that later), but it has never worked out for me to visit Victoria Falls, which would be second on my bucket list. The Falls are in the heart of Africa and are supposed to be spectacular. My daughter, Amanda, has said she would go with me, but we have not yet been able to schedule the trip. I know it will be fantastic.

The last part of this answer might sound strange, but Ulaanbaatar, Mongolia, is next on my list, and I hope to make a side trip there during a future Asia trip. Several years ago, Amanda spent a summer in Mongolia, which was a catalyst for me to read about the country, including a couple of books about Genghis Khan. I even had plans to visit Mongolia with Amanda; however, the trip ultimately had to be canceled for a reason I don't remember.

Some of my most interesting trips have been service trips. We'll explore more about service and how it's tied to being a learner in the next chapter!

Reflections

- There are so many amazing places around the world.
- Great food too!

Chapter 3

Service Trips

So, Correct Craft takes employees around the world?
Yes, we do.

Is it tough work? *Usually.*

Is it worth it? *Absolutely.*

Joining Correct Craft in late 2006 as the fifth CEO in five years, I knew there was a lot of work to do. The company was struggling mightily and needed to make bold moves. We needed to focus on building great boats, providing stellar service, and making money, but we also needed something even bigger than those goals. We needed to develop a great company culture, and it was important to me that we create a culture of service. Serving others and learning about their circumstances and lives is an important element of being a learner, too, and I believed we would not only help others but also help ourselves develop a highly effective team.

Over the years, our Correct Craft team has served many places. We have been to the Dominican Republic building a school playground, the British West Indies and Puerto Rico doing hurricane relief, and Jamaica, where we did construction at a school. We have also worked hard to serve in our local communities around the U.S. Our team has paid for and built several homes with Habitat for Humanity, provided hurricane relief in Florida, conducted lake clean-ups, and worked in homeless shelters and orphanages among many other projects. I am very blessed to be part of an amazing team—there is none better.

A culture of service helps our team realize that there was something bigger than ourselves and helps us use our platform to make the world better. In fact, that notion eventually would become our company "why," which is "Making Life Better."

While we would certainly do a lot of local community service in the years ahead, I also wanted to do something that was bold and rare for a company to do. I wanted to take our team around the world to serve in places and help people who really needed our help. It would be expensive, but there were huge rewards if we did it right; rewards to both those we were serving and those willing to serve. Fortunately, many of our employees embraced both our effort to improve Correct Craft and the new focus on service.

We didn't yet realize the adventures ahead.

The First Service Trip

The night before our first service trip, which was to Tecate, Mexico, I looked at the weather report and saw that the temperature while we would be working was going to be over 110 degrees every day. I called our HR Director, Shirley, in a panic, wondering what in the world we were doing. I had been Correct Craft CEO for just a few months, and I was taking 25 employees to the desert in Mexico to build a house in brutal heat.

The next few days in Tecate were very tough. We arrived and set up tents in the desert, but it became apparent very quickly that it was impossible to keep the sand out. Basically, we were sleeping on the desert floor.

While in Tecate, we took showers by pouring lake water over us, soaping up, and rinsing off with more lake water. Funny thing, however: After working ten hours in 110-degree heat, those cold lake water showers were some of the best I have ever enjoyed. The bathroom situation, on the other hand, was just bad—think "trench."

It was energizing to know we were building a house for one of the community's homeless families. They were a nice family of five, and we saw them every day at the worksite. They seemed very appreciative of our work. They would help us as they could, but our team was a highly focused, well-oiled machine determined to set a record for home building.

Despite our focus, the lot on which we were building the house was elevated on a small cliff, so even getting materials to the site was challenging. And unfortunately, the lot was overlooking the city sewage collection, so the smell was horrible. Sound fun?

Our team worked incredibly hard in those tough conditions and confirmed what I had been learning over my first few months at Correct Craft: We had and still have a very special team. However, despite their effort and great attitude, I wondered if they were being pushed too hard and if our first service trip would also be our last.

After completing the house, we handed the keys to the new owners in an emotional ceremony. We knew we had changed their lives in a big and positive way—we were "Making Life Better," or at least, we had for that wonderful Mexican family.

Even though handing the house keys over was a delightful experience, I knew it was a tough week and was wondering what our team really thought. While stopping in San Diego on our flight home to Florida, I had an opportunity to get the group together and ask them about the trip. I honestly wasn't sure what they would say, but I asked each person to share something with the group about their experience. Under the circumstances, I thought it was risky.

As we went around the room, each person shared their feelings about the trip. There were many misty eyes as our team made comments like "Best few days of my life," "I have never done anything so impactful," and "I cannot wait to do this again." I quickly realized that service trips would become a big part of our company culture, although not all of them were quite as challenging as our work in Tecate.

The Killing Fields

Uganda is an African country probably best known for the tyrannical leader who was its president during almost all of the 1970s, Idi Amin. Amin was going to be arrested for misappropriating funds, so as head of the country's military, he instead decided to conduct a coup that made him the nation's leader.

Uganda was a dangerous place to live before Amin, but he unleashed a complete reign of terror. By some accounts, up to 500,000 Ugandans were killed during Amin's reign, and many other citizens left the country as refugees. Fortunately for the country in general, Amin overreached by trying to annex part of neighboring Tanzania, and in 1979, Tanzanian forces ousted him from power.

After Amin left power, the killing slowed down, but things were still tough in Uganda. Even today, it is estimated that up to 1,000 people a week die from starvation and preventable disease. And, on top of that, the AIDS epidemic is devastating the country and killing hundreds more each week. One United Nations Undersecretary said that Uganda may be the worst place on earth to be a child.

Our team flew into Uganda to help. Specifically, we were there to help an organization that was providing housing and education to Ugandan kids. Upon arriving, we heard stories of workers clearing the land for the facility we were visiting and finding dozens of human skeletons that were remnants of Uganda's violent past. The kids at that facility needed help and were fortunate to have people who cared about them and had committed their lives to helping them. Our team enjoyed meeting the workers and the kids and doing what we could to help during our visit. I left Uganda praying for everyone I met and hoping that someday the country would develop in a way that would benefit its people.

Cambodia

Cambodia has a similar story as Uganda. During the late 1970s, Cambodia's communist leader, Pol Pot, set off a genocide that killed nearly two million people, or about twenty five percent of the Cambodian population. Because there was a shortage of bullets in the country, most of the killing was done by hatchet. It was a horrible situation that was only stopped when the Vietnamese army invaded the country and Pol Pot and his henchmen went on the run.

Like Uganda after the genocide, Cambodia's leader had left the country, but things were still tough in the country. The times were particularly brutal for young girls, who were captured and sexually trafficked to Western men. These men would come to Cambodia, many from the United States, specifically to exploit young girls for their pleasure.

Our team went to Cambodia to support a wakeboard cable park built outside the capital of Phnom Penh. While in the country, we saw many remnants of Cambodia's difficult past. We walked through a city previously known as "the pedophile's theme park" before a U.S. news organization sent an undercover film crew there to expose what western men were doing. We also saw exploitation that still goes on today at a brick factory where people, usually men, are sold into a lifetime of slavery because of a small debt. It is clear that people still suffer in Cambodia.

The wakeboard school we served was built specifically to provide jobs for locals and help young girls build their confidence by learning that they could excel at sport. Some of our athletes worked at the school building features for the cable park and working with the kids. We were happy to help in a place that is so desperate for something positive.

Education as a Ticket Out of Poverty

Traveling the globe, I have only needed translators on two occasions: once when I was the keynote speaker at a conference in Sao Paulo, Brazil, and once when I was meeting with government officials in Beijing, China. Almost all the educated people around the globe and the business world are multilingual and speak English. A common international joke is, "What do you call someone who only speaks one language? American."

Since English is truly the global language, it is also the "golden ticket" for those in poverty to get out of their village and into a city that will provide them upward mobility. In fact, one of the best ways to fight poverty is to educate students and specifically teach them English. Our team has been happy to support several organizations who are working hard to educate the global poor.

Ethiopia

In Ethiopia, our team traveled to a little community that had not changed much in 2,000 years. Many of the people still lived in stick huts with no electricity or bathrooms and had no modern amenities. It was apparent that the women did much of the work in the community while the men seemed to just sit around. It was very tough living, especially for the women.

However, our host was having a tremendous impact teaching the kids of the community, many who went back in the evening to teach their parents what they were learning. Our host taught not only traditional lessons and English but also valuable life skills and trades. Maybe even more impactful, they were working with the men in the community to teach them to assume some responsibility for their families and help carry the load. Our team was inspired and happy to help this wonderful organization.

Kenya

In Kenya, our service trip was very similar to Ethiopia. Our team visited some of my long-time family friends who have been working in Kenya for decades, setting up schools and orphanages. My wife and daughters had visited our friends in Kenya when my girls were teenagers. However, I had not been able to join them on that trip, so it was exciting for me to see our friend's work firsthand. They had been toiling quietly in Kenya for a long time working to make life better for people who really needed their help. Our friends are having a huge impact in Kenya, and I have said many times that people like them will be on the front row in heaven. We were happy to help them.

El Salvador

The school we have supported with the most service trips over the years is in El Salvador. Our team has taken several trips to this school and helped in many ways. We built a wall along their property line, did other construction work, painted classrooms, and built a one-of-a-kind boat in their library for the kids to have fun sitting in as they read. Another project we undertook at the school was building a computer lab, which one of our company's dealers from North Carolina helped equip with computers. This dealer was one of several vendors and dealers who have joined our team to serve globally over the years.

As a side note that was scary but fun, on one of the El Salvador trips, our team experienced an earthquake that woke us all up in the middle of the night as our rooms were shaking. For many of the team, this was a new experience, and once we realized it was not too severe, it was fun. The "El Salvador earthquake" has now become part of our service trip lore and legend.

Human Trafficking: Nicaragua and India

Serving well means learning about the good *and* the bad around the globe. Our time in Nicaragua and India exemplified that idea and had a big impact on our team.

Nicaragua

Before visiting Nicaragua, my most prevalent thought of the country involved the communist government of Daniel Ortega and the Iran Contra controversy of the 1980s. That changed when Correct Craft learned of an organization in the country that needed our help, leading us to send a team there on a service trip.

As is common in many places around the globe, girls and women are not highly valued in Nicaragua. This results in many young girls being put out of the house as pre-teens or early teens with no skills and no way to support themselves. As our service trip host explained it, many of these girls become caught up in human trafficking, which almost always leads to severe sexual abuse.

Our host in the country had a wonderful facility that takes in these young girls and teaches them a trade. For about $100, they can teach the young girls to make baskets or clothes, sell fruit, or learn another trade and give them the inventory they need to get their businesses started. By having a trade, these girls were much less vulnerable to predators who would like to use them for nefarious purposes. We were happy to spend a few days there helping with construction projects at the facility and giving back to assist these girls in a small way.

We try to spend an evening on our service trips learning about the country, and this often involves travelling to some interesting sites. While in Nicaragua, we visited the top of a local volcano. I have an iconic picture of my daughters, who had joined me on this trip, with its interior behind them. We also visited a bat cave (no, not that one) in Nicaragua where each night, thousands of bats fly out and brush your face as they leave. It is always interesting to see and learn about the places we are serving, and our team enjoys these side adventures.

Unfortunately, Nicaragua can also be a dangerous place, and we had armed guards protect the house in which we were staying. Just a short time after our trip, one of those guards was killed when intruders robbed the same house where we had stayed. Our team was shaken when we learned about the killing, but it did not reduce our resolve to travel globally and serve people who need our help.

India

While human trafficking is rampant in Nicaragua, in India, it is much worse, which our team saw first-hand. In fact, our team's trip to India served as a catalyst for us to do something we had never done: give away a boat worth over $100,000.

The root of India's problem with trafficking young girls is that many of the country's people don't value women. As a father of two wonderful girls who actually spent a couple of weeks touring India together, I could not understand stories of families mourning the birth of a daughter. This is a significant cultural problem that is deeply rooted, especially in lower castes, part of a Hindu hierarchy set up over 3,000 years ago. Women who are *dalit*—members of the lowest caste—have very little value in India's society and have a very high probability of ending up sexually trafficked. And, as we saw firsthand, it is horrifying for them.

I met our Indian host at a retreat for global non-profit leaders in Austria a couple years before our service trip to help both him and his organization. I was enthralled with the work he and his team were doing to help vulnerable young girls, and he invited me to bring a team to India to both see their work and help.

Many estimates indicate that there are millions of young girls sexually trafficked in India, with most entering the sex trade between the ages of 9 and 12. Once in the sex trade, their lives are quickly destroyed physically, mentally and emotionally. Unlike other countries that are known for sex tourism, such as Cambodia, most of the customers at Indian brothels are men from the local community who pay less than a dollar for a one-hour visit. Whether or not to use protection is at the sole discretion of the men, which obviously puts the girls at great risk. We learned much more about this horrifying situation, but it only gets worse. You get the idea, so I will spare you more details, but it is bad.

I am not comfortable naming the town and putting the organization's work at risk, but after landing in India, we were saddened to hear stories of how so many young girls end up in one of India's many red-light districts. The short version is that parents of the girls give up their daughters willingly to someone who travels to their village making false promises about providing the girl a job. The girls leave the village, and the family never hears from them again.

Our host was fighting this problem and taking a strategic approach. They are taking in vulnerable girls and promising them they would be treated as daughters. This means they help them go to college and walk them down the aisle when they get married. This lifetime commitment fixes a problem that many other well-intentioned organizations have by taking care of a girl until she turns 18 and then turning her back out on the street. Many times, even though 18 is considered too old to be "ideal," she ends up in the same brothels as those who were taken much younger.

On our first evening in India, our co-ed team went to the red-light district to see the problem firsthand. There was no attempt to hide what was happening, and we saw hundreds of brothels with young girls out front for sale. I asked our host how this was possible, and he said it was an open secret in India. It is part of the country's culture that few had the energy to fight. I saw one young girl who was just coming in from her village, and it broke my heart. I called my wife Leigh, who was back in the U.S., to tell her about the girl. Leigh's first response was, "Bring her home, we will take care of her," and if I thought there was a way to do that, I would have.

Our team was seriously impacted by what we saw. We were so impacted that we decided to donate a boat to raise both money and awareness of the problem. We built the boat with the support of several vendors and raffled it off, donating over $100,000 to fight help fight human trafficking in India. It may have only been a small amount of the total needed to fight this battle, but it was impossible for us to see what we saw in India and not want to help.

Helping People in Desperate Need

All our Correct Craft service trips have been to areas of poverty and struggling, but some areas have been worse than others.

Guatemala

Guatemala was a sobering trip for our team, as we worked in an area inhabited by the "track people." The track people were called that because they set up shanty homes on old, abandoned railroad tracks in Guatemala City. The homes consisted of old, used plywood or other disposed material stacked up to create homes. The living situation was very difficult, with many homes having an open flume of the community's sewage disposal running through their living areas.

Our team was there to help create a model bunk bed that could be used in the community, and while we did not build as many beds as we had planned, we were happy to do other work in the area and spend time getting to know the people there. Our American host in Guatemala has committed his life to helping the track people, and we were happy to support him, even in a small way.

Haiti

Our team has taken multiple trips to Pignon, Haiti, which is, again, an extremely poor area. When flying to Pignon, we chartered a WWII era DC-3 prop-plane and landed on a grass strip just outside the community. There are always locals at the landing strip excited to greet our team. Pignon is the quintessential Haitian town with people walking oxen down the dirt roads and some using the local river for a toilet while others do their laundry just downstream.

Our first trip to Pignon was to deliver food to several organizations who would distribute it throughout the community. It was a weekend trip, and our team was honored to attend a Sunday morning church service in the community. It was humbling to see so many people walking long distances down dirt roads in their Sunday best to be with their spiritual family. Later, on other trips, we took a couple of different groups back to Pignon to make improvements to one of the community's schools.

In the spirit of service trips never being boring, it was on one of the later trips to Pignon that we went out into the countryside to deliver food and got caught in a bad rainstorm. Being from Florida, we are used to rainstorms, but not when driving on dirt roads that are not maintained at all. Of course, one of our vehicles got stuck in the storm, and it was quite difficult getting it free (no AAA to call in Pignon). Several of our team ended up covered in mud from head to toe getting the truck back on the road, but it is now another great memory!

The U.S.: Apache Reservation

Our team has learned firsthand that extreme poverty is not limited to areas outside the U.S. We have also served in very high-poverty areas of our own country, including the Apache reservation and Winthrop, California.

On the first of what would be two trips to build a home in the Apache reservation about three hours outside of Phoenix, it was hard to believe what we were seeing actually existed in the United States. There have been plenty of books written about the genocide of Native Americans, the Trail of Tears, and other struggles the first Americans have endured, but seeing the poverty many endure today firsthand was sobering.

Many of America's poorest one percent live in one of the over three hundred Indian reservations throughout the U.S. A combination of minimal property rights since much of the land is owned communally, hesitancy of U.S. business to work on reservations because of legal issues resulting from their unique nation status, and minimal investment on reservation infrastructure, health care, and education have resulted in extreme poverty.

On the Apache reservation where we served, the poverty rate is over fifty percent, and the extreme poverty rate is over twenty-five percent, dramatically higher than the national average. The living conditions in the Arizona desert for the Apaches are extremely tough. Our team wanted to help.

After arriving on the reservation for our first Apache service trip, we set up tents in the desert very similar to our camp in Tecate, Mexico. While setting up the tents, we did not realize that a couple days later, they would be destroyed by a freak hailstorm. Needless to say, we were surprised when returning to camp after working all day in the hundred-degree-plus desert sun to find our tents crumbled and soaking wet with chunks of ice left over from the hail still floating on our belongings.

As always, our team worked hard on the Apache reservation, and we were happy to play a small part in helping those who needed our assistance. Since service trips are always an adventure, after our work and the hailstorm, we found ourselves back in Phoenix waiting for the next morning's flight home trapped in our hotel because a huge desert sandstorm had moved in. These trips are never boring.

One of our most recent trips was to Winthrop, California, which is less than an hour from our company's plant that builds Centurion and Supreme boats. Winthrop is a poor community with a lot of immigrants and a very high poverty rate. Our team in California introduced us to the founder of the Winthrop Community Center who needed our help. About a hundred members of our team from all over the country travelled to the community center and completely refurbished it. After the work was done, we sent some of our team back to help the community center develop a long-term strategic plan.

And, in the spirit of service trips never being boring, California experienced an earthquake while we were in Winthrop. This was old hat for those who had been with us when the El Salvador earthquake struck but a new experience for many on our team.

Our Team Loves to Serve

I have said many times that if I decided to get another bachelor's degree, it would be in psychology. One thing I have found interesting as I read psychology books and articles is that the path to being happy is counter-intuitive and exactly the opposite of what we learn in many self-help books. Many books will tell us we have to love ourselves and focus on making ourselves happy and provide a litany of different ways to do that. However, this approach almost always puts us on what other psychologists call "the hedonic treadmill." Basically, this means that you can't make yourself happy. The more you try to make yourself happy, the more it just leads to brief moments of fun but not sustained joy. When these brief moments happen, the hedonic treadmill speeds up and sends us desperately looking for the next shot of happiness.

There is a tremendous amount of evidence that when we focus on others, we are genuinely happy. I have seen this over and over as our team has travelled the globe and worked under difficult circumstances to help people who have no possible way of paying them back. And it is not unusual to hear them say, like they did in that San Diego meeting after Tecate, something like, "Best few days of my life!" And all of the service members have at least one thing in common: being learners. They are all open to new experiences and new insights into how the rest of the world operates, and through that willingness, we are able to do great good.

Reflections

- People all over the world need help.

- We should use our platforms, whatever they are, to help others.

- Serving together develops great organizational culture.

- There is great joy in serving others, especially when they cannot pay you back.

Chapter 4

Things Don't Always Go According to Plan

Most of the time, travel takes place without a problem, but occasionally, there can be unexpected adventures. Anyone who travels often is likely to have unforeseen and sometimes scary experiences. I look back on each time this has happened to me as not only an adventure but also a part of my education I wouldn't trade. I have learned that not only anticipating but also embracing the unexpected often takes me out of my comfort zone, which is a very positive experience. As my friend and ex-CIA agent Michelle says, "We learn very little in our comfort zone."

Crossing Boundaries

I've talked about this before, but one of the most important things you can do for personal and professional life is push boundaries and extend outside of your comfort zone. This is true even when the experience seems overwhelming or unexpected. With that in mind, here are some stories where crossing borders didn't quite go according to plan.

3 a.m. in Tijuana

On Correct Craft's second service trip to Tecate, Mexico, I had to leave a day before the rest of the group to get back to Orlando for an important meeting. With a Sunday morning flight out of San Diego, one of the interns working with the organization helping us serve volunteered to get up at 2 a.m. and drive me from Tecate to the San Diego airport. This required driving through Tijuana and crossing the border at 3 a.m. on a Saturday night. Needless to say, this was not well thought-out.

When we arrived in Tijuana, there were hundreds of cars lined up to cross the border into the U.S., most of them filled with inebriated Americans who had come into Mexico for some Saturday-night fun and who were now going home. The intern guessed it would take at least three hours to cross the border, which would result in me missing my flight to Florida, but she also had another idea. Apparently, as a frequent border crosser, she had some sort of "fast pass" that allowed her to drive through the border crossing without stopping. The only catch was that I was not allowed to cross with her. So, at 3 a.m. on a Saturday night, she dropped me off in Tijuana, about a hundred yards from the border, so I could walk across. The decision to get out of the car led to ten of the scariest minutes of my life.

I wanted to leave my backpack in the vehicle, but the intern said that I was required to keep it with me. Without telling her, I took my laptop out and threw it on the car's back seat floor, thinking that if my backpack was stolen, at least I would have my computer.

Immediately after getting out of the car, I knew it was a very big mistake. Drunk people were all yelling at me, and many of the locals were calling me pejorative names that I won't write. It was clear I was in a very rough area of town, and everyone was seemingly drunk. As I started walking toward the border, a local man came up and started walking next to me, literally bumping up against me with every step. He kept asking me questions which I tried to answer as succinctly as possible, trying not to engage with him but also trying not to enrage him by being disrespectful.

As we were walking by very drunk and passed-out people laying around, he kept asking me why I was in Mexico—it was a surreal sight and experience. Thinking, mistakenly, that somehow it would help, I finally told him I was in Mexico to help build a house for a homeless family. He apparently didn't like that idea and loudly replied for the drunken crowd around us to hear, "Oh, yeah, rich American coming down to help the poor Mexicans, huh?" Unfortunately, my plan to make nice had backfired, and he began bumping me harder and harder with each step.

Finally, he bumped me extra hard and—I am not making this up—said, "You know, I have killed people," to which I wanted to respond with a bit of sarcastic machismo that I had killed people, too, before deciding it was wiser not to reply. For clarity's sake, I don't recall ever killing anyone, so I am pretty sure it would have been a lie anyway.

Thankfully, as we got very close to the border, he peeled off, but the area around the border gate was not much better. There were dozens of drunk people screaming obscenities at the immigration officials, and I remember thinking that they would have to pay me a lot of money to be a border guard there.

Unfortunately for me, as I got close to the border, before the walk-and-bump killer had left me, I had a mishap that has rarely happened to me in over thirty years of wearing contact lenses. The contact in one of my eyes rolled up, causing me pain. It also made my eye bright red and created a steady flow of tears from the irritation. Not that I needed something else to make me stand out.

When I finally made it up to the immigration agent, he was a little suspicious of this seemingly sober guy walking across the border at 3 a.m. with just a backpack, bright red eye, and tears flowing. After looking at my passport, the first thing he said to me was, "So, what's up with your eye?" to which I tried to explain what was occurring and how this very rarely happens to me. After I explained the situation to him and why I was crossing the border at 3 a.m., he eventually let me back in the U.S., but I am sure he must have thought I was crazy.

After passing through immigration and customs, the environment on the U.S. side of the border was a little better, but not by much. I saw the intern's car waiting for me about a block ahead, but as I got closer to her, she drove off, not seeing me and afraid of getting in trouble for parking illegally. This situation was now really crazy.

Fortunately, I reached the intern on her cell phone and she drove around the block to pick me up. Sitting down in the passenger seat as she drove off was an incredible relief. I learned that I never again wanted to cross the border in Tijuana at 3 a.m.

Crossing the Israeli–Jordan border

Tijuana was not the only time I had a scary adventure walking across a border. The second time was in the Middle East walking across the border from Israel to Jordan. While Jordan and Israel signed a peace treaty in 1994, there still seemed to be some tension between the countries, and the border area felt a little more stressful than most.

The Israeli cab driver dropped me, one of our company sales reps, and one of our team athletes off at the Israeli border so we could process through the Rabin border terminal in Israel before walking a couple hundred yards to the Araba border station in Jordan. I needed to get into Jordan to fly into some other Middle Eastern countries that cannot be accessed directly from Israel.

Normally, this border crossing would be uneventful, but I was travelling with two passports and wanted to enter Israel with one passport and enter Jordan with another. Entering Jordan from Israel is perfectly fine, and the Jordanians obviously saw me walking to Jordan from Israel, but I would later be travelling to other Middle Eastern countries that frowned on an Israeli stamp in visitor's passports. So, I kept two passports to avoid trouble at future border crossings.

My two travelling companions who were not going to all the same countries as me passed through Jordanian customs and immigration with no issues, but I was the third of our group to go through, and as I found out, it was going to be a challenge.

After taking my passport, the Jordanian immigration officer got a real serious look on his face as he was keypunching away on his computer, apparently checking my travel history. He kept hitting keys, and what had been a couple-minute process for my colleagues was becoming a long process for me, and he had that serious look on his face.

The officer spoke very poor English, and I spoke no Arabic, so that didn't help. Finally, he motioned for me to follow him to a back room, which I (correctly) assumed was not a good sign. You don't have to be a seasoned traveler to know getting called to the "back room" in this situation is not what you want to see. Once there, he introduced me to his co-worker (or at least I think that's what he did), who took my passport and started keypunching away on his computer with an equally serious look. I was getting nervous. My colleagues were waiting out in the sun so we could walk to the Jordanian border town and catch a cab to Amman.

After a lot of keypunching and more serious looks, the back-room guy motioned for me to follow him to another room. Once there, a third immigration officer began looking at my passport, keypunching, and quickly took on the very serious look of the previous two officers. The third man, who I believe was a supervisor, finally looked up at me and asked in perfect English, "Do you have another passport?" This was the question I did not want.

I responded yes, of course, and he asked to see it. I dug deep in my backpack to retrieve it, and I handed the passport over as he did some more keypunching with the same serious look. I wondered if this happened often and wished I knew Arabic so I could tell him a joke. You know, to lighten the mood a little.

Finally, he looked up and told me I needed to enter Jordan with the same passport that I had used to enter Israel. This would have been a big problem for me because every country I visited on the rest of my Middle East trip would want to know how I got into the previous country before visiting them. Some countries don't like it if you have visited Israel, so stamping the wrong passport would throw a big monkey wrench into my trip because the other countries were not likely to admit me if they saw I had come from Israel. The immigration agent now had both of my passports in front of him and told me he was going to stamp the wrong one.

I respectfully asked him to stamp the one that would not mess up my future travel, and he told me that he needed to stamp the one I had used to enter Israel. This went back and forth a few times. I had suspicions as to why he kept telling me that and what he might want, but I definitely wasn't going there. I kept respectfully, but firmly, asking him to stamp the other one that I needed for the rest of my trip. Finally, he gave me an angry look and barked something in Arabic but stamped the one I needed him to stamp. He roughly tossed both passports back at me, and I left happily, heading to find my colleagues and a cab for Amman.

I learned to always expect the process to go a little longer when you are crossing a border on foot.

Addis Ababa to New Delhi

Leaving a service trip in Ethiopia on the way to Kuala Lumpur, Malaysia, for the Asian Waterski and Wakeboard championships, which our company was sponsoring, required an overnight trip to change planes in New Delhi, India. Traveling with one of our team, we were the only passengers on the Ethiopian Airlines plane who were not part of a Chinese construction crew going home after working to help build a highway in Ethiopia.

The plane was scheduled to leave Addis Ababa around about 11 p.m. for the eight-hour flight to India, and the rowdiness was beginning already at the gate. I wondered if the flight would go on, as the construction workers had clearly already begun celebrating their trip home. A lot of alcohol was involved.

The plane was a wide-body, and we were sitting in the middle section of the exit row, so there was a row of seats missing in front of us. Unfortunately, this just put us on the racetrack for a night full of lapping around the plane by its passengers.

There was yelling, shouting, and of course, a lot more drinking. No one was even trying to sleep on the overnight trip. Because we were on the racetrack, people were climbing over us all night as they raced around the plane. Some of the workers clearly did not like each other, but since I really had no idea what they were saying, that was just my perception based on their body language and tone of voice. Whatever they were saying, it was clearly not nice, and several times on the flight, I was concerned a fight would break out.

I was also concerned that Ethiopian Airlines would ground the flight before we got to New Delhi, which would have really messed up our travel plans. We made it to New Delhi okay, and presumably, the Chinese highway workers made their connection and got back home. I guess we all like to let loose a little while heading home for vacation after working hard for months in another country. I cannot imagine what their next flight was like.

Adapting to Curveballs

Physical boundaries aren't the only boundaries you'll face while traveling and learning about the world, of course. I want to talk about some of the other unexpected experiences I've encountered while traveling.

Water Pipe in Antigua

The Antigua Yacht Charter Show was a favorite event for our customers in the 1990s, so I took off with a colleague to see what it
was all about. Arriving at the airport in Antigua, we realized the
show was on the other side of the island, and the rental car attendant told us we had two options: We could stay on the main road
around the island, or we could go over the top of the mountains for
the more interesting route to our destination. The rental car was at
least fifteen years old and all beat up, but it was an easy decision—
we were going over the mountains.

In the mountains, going through a heavily wooded area, one of
us needed to make a quick "pit stop," and since we were in what
I thought was the middle of nowhere, we just pulled over. As I was
pulling over, I felt us run over something. The next thing we knew,
water started shooting at least ten feet in the air in front of the car.

With no idea what was happening, a man appeared out of
nowhere and started yelling at us, saying that we had run over
the water line to the "village." That didn't sound good, and I had
no idea what village he was talking about but assumed there was
one nearby. Within minutes, a group of islanders had surrounded
us and, frankly, I had no idea what to do. They were unhappy, as I
would have been had someone just run over the water line into my
house.

Finally, they told us to let the people in the next village know
and sent us on our way. I wasn't sure what the people of the next
village would do, but we found an official who seemed to be an
authority and let him know. The village where we found the official
had very narrow streets and cars parked on both sides of the road,
which made driving through it perilous. We did okay with that until
I was going just a little too fast as the road narrowed, and I heard a
smash. I quickly realized that I had just hit a van and taken off the

driver's side mirror of our rental car. We were less than two hours into our Antigua trip, but it was off to an interesting start.

After arriving at the Yacht Charter Show, the next couple of days in Antigua were spectacular, and I quickly realized why our yachting customers liked being there. The harbor surrounded by mountains was breathtaking. On the way back to the airport, we decided it would be smart to take the direct route around the mountain and avoid the over-the-top experience of the mountain path. We arrived at the airport with a car that was missing a mirror, but other than that, we were okay. That is, until the rental car clerk started getting a serious look on his face, just like the immigration officials had in Jordan.

The clerk kept keypunching and looking at his computer very seriously before finally looking up at me and saying, "We have a problem." Given our adventure getting over the mountain, I was a little concerned about what the problem could be. Finally, he said we had not put enough gas in the car and that for $6 he could make the problem go away. I gave him a $10 bill and told him to "keep the change" and was happy to get on the plane for Florida.

A Day in the Cayman Islands

In the 1980s, newly married Leigh and I decided to do something that even today we have only done once, though we have probably had it offered to us dozens of times. We took a timeshare sales tour and listened to their presentation in exchange for a three-day trip to the Cayman Islands.

The timeshare tour was interesting, but we had no money and were not going to finance a timeshare, which I told the salesman immediately, but he insisted on giving us the presentation, and we kept up our end of the deal by listening carefully. No matter how appealing the timeshare sounded, we still did not have any money at the end of the meeting, so the salesman gave us our vacation information, and we were on our way. We had lost two hours, but were headed to the Cayman Islands.

We made our plans, and finally, the day came for our trip. The flight was uneventful, and I was fascinated as we flew over communist Cuba, not realizing that a couple of decades later, I would be visiting that very island on a trade mission. We landed on the island, and all was well until we got to our hotel. It was a dump. The hotel was in a bad section of town, not near the water, and it had a bunch of locals sitting outside who did not greet us with "island hospitality." When we got to our room, it was filthy, and I am not exaggerating, green water ran out of the sink. The locals were walking back and forth by our room, and the worst part was that the door to our room had wood slats with one missing so anyone could literally reach their hand through the slat and open the door, even if it was locked. Being new to international travel, we were not feeling good about our trip or hotel.

Even though we could not afford it, I started calling other hotels only to realize we were there during the annual Cayman Islands Pirates Week, so there was not an available room on the island. This was the first time either of us had been out of the U.S., so we were not comfortable at all and decided to fly home immediately. Fortunately, the airline could accommodate us, and we made it home that day. However, this was the "drug running" 1980s, so we did get some extra attention coming back into the U.S., especially since we came back the same day we had left.

Our family has been back to the Cayman Islands, and it is a spectacular place that we would highly recommend. There you can swim with stingrays, horseback ride on the beach, and our family really enjoyed snorkeling the wreck of the Cali. However, I learned on this trip that it's not a great idea to let a timeshare company book your hotel, especially when you didn't buy their product.

Fertility Clinic in Morocco

Several years ago, while I was serving on a council advising the U.S. Secretary of Commerce, our company was also working with the U.S. Department of Commerce (DOC) to help us find distributors around the world. One of the places the DOC looked into was Morocco.

I was invited to attend an international conference on doing business with Morocco at the same time we were ready to meet with some of the distributors the DOC was suggesting could help us. So, I flew to Rabat, Morocco's capital, for an interesting conference. I always enjoy meeting leaders from different businesses, industries, and parts of the world. I was even invited to a reception at the U.S. ambassador's home! It was a fascinating couple of days.

After the conference in Rabat, I travelled to Casablanca where I connected with one of our company's international team members who had flown to Morocco to join me in meeting the potential distributors. After arriving, we went to the U.S. Consulate in Casablanca to meet our contact. The security was substantially tougher than getting into the White House. We met with the in-country DOC representative who was helping us find distributors, and we made our plans for the next day.

Our first meeting with a potential distributor was at 9 a.m., so we, not really being sure where the meeting was being held, left the hotel early in a cab. We handed the cab driver our desired destination on a piece of paper, which is always a smart thing to do if you don't speak the language and the driver does not speak English. The driver dropped us off in front of a building that had the right number on the front, pointed to the building, and we went inside at about 8:30 a.m.

Our meeting was in Suite 310, but there was a reception desk on the ground floor where we checked in, so we handed the lady a card with the name of the person we were supposed to see. She acknowledged the card, so we sat and waited, not getting any indication when or if someone would come for us. We did, however, curiously see a lot of medical workers and people bringing in carts of flowers and large gift baskets. But it was a five-story building, so it seemed logical that there could be different types of offices in the space.

As it got close to 9 a.m. with no response, we were getting nervous, and since the receptionist did not appear to speak English, we decided to take the elevator to the third floor ourselves and find the person with whom we were supposed to meet. In the elevator, the other passengers were dressed in medical attire, but we did not think much about it.

Upon arriving on the third floor, we noticed that the hallways were lined with the gift baskets and flowers that we had seen being carted in while we waited in the lobby. Because the doors were not labeled, however, we had no idea where our potential distributor might be. So, I decided to pop in one of the doors and ask for help. Big mistake.

I tapped lightly on one of the doors and then opened it to ask for help. To my surprise, there was a lady lying on a table with her feet in stirrups waiting for what would clearly be a medical examination. I quickly tried to say I am sorry, she screamed, and I bolted.

Coming out of the room, I told my colleague to follow me, and we ran down the stairs since we were definitely not waiting for the elevator. We ran out of the building into the city street and found someone who spoke English. Much to our chagrin, we were told that we had just come out of a fertility clinic. Deciding we should get away as fast as possible, we found someone to direct us to the right address. We eventually reached the right place and apologized for arriving late to our meeting.

Flying into the Maldives

One of our company's international sales reps joined me and others from our team on a service trip to India, and since I was already in the area, he asked if I would join him for meetings in Sri Lanka and the Maldives. After the service trip, we travelled to Sri Lanka, having a good visit there with a ski school before moving on to the Maldives to visit a prospective distributor.

I had heard a lot about the Maldives and once even sat next to a nice lady on a flight who was telling me the Maldives was her dream vacation destination. We were only going to be in the islands for one day, but I was interested to see them, or at least the one we were visiting. That is, until I got nervous on our flight to the country.

The Maldives is a conservative Muslim country, which is interesting because it is also known as a global beach resort destination. However, that did not concern me because I had travelled to many conservative countries before and am always respectful of my hosts. But on the short two-hour flight from Sri Lanka to the Maldives, the airline gave me a paper that caused me great concern.

The airline's paper listed several things that visitors were prohibited from bringing into the country by penalty of death. Yep, you read that right, *death*. Some of the items on the paper included guns, pork, pornography, idols for worship, anything anti-Islam, narcotics, or steroids. After reading the list and thinking carefully if I might have any pork snacks in my bag, I wasn't worried except for the last two items noted above: narcotics and steroids.

The general international rule for bringing drugs into a country is that it is okay if the drugs are in a prescription bottle specifically prescribed to the traveler. I was in compliance with this rule and had previously travelled to some very conservative countries without concern. However, I had never received a paper from an airline talking about "death" for a violation. I knew it was unlikely they would execute a U.S. citizen, but we all know crazier things have happened.

I had legitimate prescription drugs in my backpack, but I was worried they fell under the "death penalty" category. Every few years, I tend to get very painful kidney stones, and I had some pain medicine from my last kidney stone adventure in my backpack in case they flared up again and I needed some relief until getting home to a hospital. The pain medicine was legitimate, and the bottle had my name on it.

Another lifelong malady of mine is severe allergies, and every couple of years they get so bad that the only relief I get is from some prednisone I kept with me, again, a legitimate though rarely used prescription in a bottle with my name. I am a pretty risk-tolerant guy, and I thought my risk going into the Maldives was low, but I also knew the potential consequences were very high.

An hour into the two-hour flight, I was getting really nervous. I decided I needed to do something, and I knew I needed to do it fast. My backpack with the prescriptions was in the overhead storage, so I got up to retrieve it, and for some reason, I decided that it wasn't smart to be seen with the prescription bottles, so I took the entire backpack into the lavatory. Nothing suspicious about that.

Once in the lavatory, I took the pills out of the bottle and threw them into the bottom of the toilet and flushed. The airplane toilet flushed, but there is little if any water flow, and the pills stayed right where they were, stuck to the toilet flap. Not wanting to touch the pills in the bottom of the toilet to push them down, I started using my hands to cup water from the faucet and throw it into the toilet to loosen the pills off the flap so they would flush, and thankfully, they eventually did.

I had managed to lose the pills but, now, what to do with the bottles? After thinking about it, I decided they would not execute me for empty pill bottles, so instead of throwing them in the plane's garbage with my personal information on the label, I decided it was safer to return them to my backpack.

After landing in the Maldives, I passed through immigrations and customs without officers even looking in my backpack, so I likely would have been fine. But 35,000 feet in the air between Sri Lanka and the Maldives, I could not be sure, and when death is involved, I lose my risk tolerance.

Attempted Robbery in Cairo

Travelling to Egypt a year or so after the 2011 revolution resulted in my scariest travelling adventure. The country was still reeling from the violent revolution, and driving to the revolution's epicenter, Tahrir Square, my host and I passed burned-out government buildings. Tahrir Square was quiet the day we visited, and everything seemed peaceful on that beautiful, sunny day.

After the Tahrir square visit and lunch, which was the second meal we shared on the bank of the Nile River, my host wanted to take me to Giza to view the pyramids and the sphinx. He insisted that no trip to Cairo would be complete without visiting their most popular tourist site. I was fascinated with the pyramids and the thought of seeing them, and the sphinx intrigued me, so I did not put up much of an argument against going.

Driving through Cairo, the streets were exactly as you would likely imagine in a Middle Eastern metropolis. They were narrow and crowded with many shops displaying their goods on the sidewalk, giving off a marketplace vibe. It was a fun cultural experience until two men stepped out in front of our car and my host slammed on the brakes to keep from hitting them. As soon as we stopped, several other men surrounded the car, shouting to us in Arabic. I had no idea what they were saying but assumed it was not good. I pictured myself on CNN holding up a newspaper to verify the date.

My host rolled his window down just about an inch, and the men kept yelling at us. There were also lots of hand waving. Finally, my host started slowly pulling forward, and the men in front of the car were walking and then jogging backward to keep from getting run over. As we kept speeding up, I was sure my host was just going to run over the guys in front of us until they finally jumped out of the way. One of the other guys jumped on the back of the car as we pulled away. I could plainly see his face screaming at us as we navigated the narrow and crowded street. Finally, we turned a corner, and I watched as the guy holding onto the back of our car was literally thrown off the car into the crowd on the busy street.

Moral of the story? Don't be afraid to take risks and push yourself out of your comfort zone. That's one way learners thrive. With that said, maybe look up crimes punishable by death before getting on a plane to a new country.

Reflections

-   People who travel will have interesting experiences.
-   There is risk in almost everything we do, including travel.
-   Those who are willing to get out of their comfort zone benefit greatly.

Chapter 5

Politics

Like everyone else, I have political opinions but for a bunch of reasons have pretty much kept them to myself. As a reader and a bit of a news junkie, I have always been interested in politics. Interestingly enough, this is likely one of the best examples of where being a learner has benefitted me that I could give. A decade ago, I thought I had a good idea of how the system worked, but looking back, I realize that I had no idea. I didn't even have a clue about the education and information I would receive traveling to Washington D.C. dozens of times and working for both the Trump and Obama administrations. I've had to learn a lot over the past ten years, and if I hadn't been open to exploring new ideas and situations, I never would have found myself in some pretty incredible situations.

Politics Are Global

South Korea

In the spring of 2011, while having lunch with South Korean officials at the Seoul Olympic Village, I had no idea how much that meeting was going to change my life. South Korea was the second stop—just after Japan—of a two-and-a-half-week whirlwind Asian business trip that had me and one of our team visiting several different countries where we met a lot of people, both in and out of government.

We were trying to develop relationships with potential Asian distributors, and the meetings in South Korea were all typical business meetings that went well. Other than the team member I was travelling with being bothered by our hosts repeatedly putting their chopsticks into his stew to pull out something they wanted him to appreciate, the meal was uneventful.

After returning to Orlando from the Asia trip, I received an unexpected call from the South Korean embassy in Washington, D.C. They said that former South Korean Prime Minister and then-Ambassador to the U.S. Han Duck-soo had heard about my visit to South Korea and wanted to fly to Orlando and meet. Obviously, the call was surprising, but it was an honor, so we set up a day to spend together in Orlando. The day included meetings with our team and a tour of our Orlando facility before we rode together to downtown Orlando for a joint press conference on doing business in South Korea. The press conference was important because the U.S. Senate was considering the Obama administration's U.S. Korea Free Trade Agreement (KORUS), which our industry supported.

Ambassador Han had a great day in Orlando and enjoyed both the tour of our Nautique plant and the meetings with our team. The press conference with the ambassador, which was my first press conference, also went well, and I was happy it ended without me creating an international incident. We had great chemistry, and throughout the day, I grew to respect Ambassador Han. At the end of the day, he gave me a tie that his wife had made before we shook hands and agreed to stay in touch. But of course, we didn't stay in touch—we were both busy guys.

Until, that is, I heard later that year that Ambassador Han had been invited to meet President Obama in the Oval Office prior to signing the recently ratified KORUS agreement. And he wanted me to go with him. Hearing that on a Wednesday night was interesting, especially since the Oval Office meeting was only about 36 hours later. Of course, I cleared my schedule and the next afternoon flew to Washington, D.C. for the Friday-morning meeting with the President.

The Oval Office

Arriving at the White House and getting through security was an adventure. I have been to the White House many times since, but that first visit to meet the president, in the Oval Office no less, was the only time I have had an issue with security. The meeting with the president was scheduled for 9 a.m., so I was told to be there no later than 8:45 a.m. to get through security. I decided to take no chances and walked up to the gate outside the West Wing around 8:15 a.m. and presented my identification to the guard. He looked at his list of Oval Office guests for the day and promptly told me I was not on it; now that was surprising. I have done some fast talking in my day, but it is not surprising that you cannot smooth-talk your way into the Oval Office.

I was confused since I had spoken to one of the president's staff several times the day before while working with him to make arrangements for the visit. I asked the guard if he would call my contact, but he told me he wasn't allowed to do that. When I called my contact's cell phone, which the day before he had always answered on the first ring, there was no response. I called my executive assistant in Orlando and asked her to go on the White House website and call any number she could find and ask to speak to my contact. Time was ticking away, and I was getting concerned until, about 8:40 a.m., the guard called me back to his desk stating the staffer had called and cleared me to go in. He apologized for the mistake, and after I passed through security, the guard pointed me toward the West Wing, and I walked up the White House driveway unescorted to meet the president.

Walking in the West Wing lobby, I saw Ambassador Han already there, and I sat next to him so we could catch up. We took a picture together for which we got a prompt scolding, since apparently no pictures were allowed in the West Wing lobby, and we waited to meet the President. After a few minutes, and after putting our phones in cubby holes to keep us from bringing them into the Oval

Office, we were escorted around the corner to the Roosevelt Room where we waited with a few other business leaders who were there for the KORUS signing.

Finally, the time came to walk into the Oval Office, and the President was waiting to greet each of us, so I walked up to him and said, "Hello, Mr. President, I am Bill Yeargin." The President had obviously been well-briefed because, to my surprise, he said, "I know who you are, and your company builds great boats." He then went on to tell me his daughters had been to a summer camp that had our boats, and when the girls got back from camp, the boats were all they wanted to talk about. We talked about wake surfing, and I invited him to try it with me next time he was in Florida. He joked that he was too old for that, and I responded that we were about the same age and if I could do it, surely, he could.

The President bantered a bit with us and then signed the KORUS agreement. I thought it was interesting that he signed every letter of his name with a different pen, while he was assuring us it was legal, so there would be several "signing pens" to hand out. I was hoping he would give the pens to those of us in the room, but he didn't; I guess the Oval Office pictures were souvenirs enough. Since no cell phones were allowed in the Oval Office, all the pictures were taken by the White House photographer, who later sent me one with President Obama laughing while I told him he could wake surf. It is a neat memento.

After signing the agreement, we walked out into the White House Rose Garden where a few dozen people were waiting for us (actually, I am pretty sure they were just waiting for him), and the President made some remarks about the agreement but, unfortunately, he did not mention our boats again. After his remarks, the President mingled with the group in the Rose Garden, and I decided to meet as many of the people as possible, greeting and making friends with various CEOs, ambassadors, and cabinet secretaries. It was a fun and memorable day.

A short time after the Oval Office meeting, I was surprised to learn that Ambassador Han had resigned to move back to Seoul and become Chair of the Korean International Trade Association. While I was surprised Ambassador Han was leaving, I was even more surprised when I was invited to speak at the welcoming ceremony for the new South Korean ambassador, Choi Young-jin, who I had never met. The event was hosted by the U.S. Chamber of Commerce, and there were only two speakers, me and the U.S. Trade Representative, Ambassador Ron Kirk. It had only been a year since that lunch in Seoul, but a lot had happened and, in some ways, it seemed a lifetime ago.

During the balance of the Obama Administration, I was invited back to the White House four more times after my Oval Office meeting. One time was to discuss national infrastructure, another time to discuss free trade, and twice more to discuss ways the government could support U.S. manufacturing. No matter how many times I go to the White House, it always provides an incredible sense of awe.

A little over a year after the Oval Office visit, I was asked to serve on the Manufacturing Council, a group of about twenty-five business leaders who advise the U.S. Secretary of Commerce. Penny Pritzker, the Commerce Secretary during most of my time on the Council, was very sharp and seemed interested in our counsel. The first couple of years on the Manufacturing Council, I served on the Innovation Committee, and the last couple of years, I was honored to co-chair the Tax and Trade Committee. The Council and our committees worked hard, and I believed we offered the Secretary and President good advice.

During the Obama Administration, I met one of the President's staff, a nice lady who managed the President's Advisory Council on Africa. We were seated together at a dinner and had a long conversation about Africa. I had been to Africa several times and had some strong thoughts about what I saw happening there and, especially, what China was doing on the continent (more on that later). After our conversation, she asked me if I would be interested on serving the President on his Advisory Council for Africa, but I was disappointed that nothing came out of it.

Political Change

While I tried very hard not to be "political," I realized the election would bring changes and was not sure if my Washington D.C. work would continue with the new Administration. But it did.

Working with the Trump Administration began when I was contacted by Vice President Pence's office about him visiting our Orlando plant, which I wrote about in an earlier chapter. After that visit, I stayed in contact with the Vice President's office and was honored later when they asked me to sit on a roundtable at an event he was attending in Jacksonville, Florida, regarding the United States–Mexico–Canada Free Trade Agreement (USMCA). It was also fun to be invited to greet the V.P. on the tarmac when he flew into our area for a visit to the Kennedy Space Center. That meeting was particularly fun because I was able to invite some of our team, and Pence's staff gave us a tour of Air Force Two.

The Trump Administration's first Secretary of the Interior, Ryan Zinke, invited me to serve on the Outdoor Recreation Advisory Council (ORAC), a group of business leaders who advised him, and of course, I was honored to do it. Later, I became Chair of that Council, but it was eventually terminated when the President issued an executive order requiring his cabinet to reduce the number of advisory councils. The purpose of reducing the number of advisory councils was financial, but my experience demonstrated that the councils provided some very high-caliber business leaders who were willing to work for free; it seemed like a good deal for the government to me.

History Repeats Itself

During the Trump Administration, I was invited to the White House three times.

The first time was to meet with one of the White House Chief Economists about the global trade war. I had been very vocal in writing about trade war's impact on U.S. businesses such as ours and have testified before the International Trade Commission in opposition to some of the administration's tariffs. So, I really appreciated the White House being interested in hearing my view. The meeting was actually held in Vice President Pence's ceremonial office, and though he was not there, it was fun to get a picture sitting at his desk.

The desk was originally used in the Oval Office before JFK brought in the Resolute desk, but later, Nixon moved this particular desk back into the Oval Office when he was president: It was the desk in which he had the hidden tape recorder. I looked but did not see any stray recording equipment or tapes, though the desk was signed by many who had used it, including Truman, Eisenhower, Mondale, Quayle, Bush, and Cheney. Though he used it, the desk was not signed by Nixon—they said he left town in a bit of a rush.

While Chair of the Outdoor Recreation Advisory Council, I was invited back to the White House again to hear President Trump describe his administration's policies on outdoor recreation. It was an interesting meeting that included several CEOs, cabinet secretaries, and some of the President's staff, including his daughter, Ivanka.

My third invite to the Trump White House was unfortunately cancelled when the President contracted COVID-19. That trip, I was bringing two of our company's boats with me to show the President, so I was really disappointed.

In the fall of 2019, President Trump gave a presentation to the United Nations on religious liberty, and I was one of a handful of business leaders who were invited by the White House to attend. I was happy to be at the United Nations on a day that the U.S. President was standing up for those persecuted around the world because of their religious faith.

Finally, in the summer of 2020, our team was happy to host the Trump Administration's Secretary of Interior, David Bernhardt, at our Orlando headquarters. I appreciated the opportunity to tell Secretary Bernhardt about both our company and our industry's substantive economic impact. Our team gave the Secretary a plant tour, a preview of our electric boat, and both a wake surfing and wakeboarding demonstration. It was a fun day.

Politics Should Not Be a Team Sport

During the years of working with both the Obama and Trump Administrations, I also had a fair bit of interaction with Congress on Capitol Hill. Meeting with Congressional Representatives of both parties was interesting, and they always seemed gracious and happy to meet. I was even invited by one congressman to climb to the top of the Capitol Rotunda, an adventure not available to the public and something I didn't even realize could be done. The views of the Capitol Mall looking down past the Washington Monument toward the Lincoln Memorial were spectacular from the top of the Rotunda.

Outside the U.S., I have had a few interesting encounters with political leaders, and while we generally tend to just see them through the television camera, I am always struck by how normal most of them are.

Once arriving at the airport in Tallinn, Estonia, for a flight to Helsinki, Finland, I found it odd that the plane had a red carpet lined with military as we all boarded the back of the aircraft. Once on, it was also odd that the passengers only filled the front half of the plane and the back half was empty. However, soon after we boarded, a motorcade drove up and some dignified officials greeted it as some more dignified officials got out of the motorcade and boarded our plane. Once the dignitaries got on the plane, the flight attendant told me we were flying with the President of Hungary. I thought it unusual that he did not have his own plane and even more unusual that he was flying in the back of the plane.

I have been honored to meet the Crown Prince of Dubai when our team delivered a new Nautique boat to him, which was interesting since his picture was all around town. My host in Bahrain arranged for us to meet with the President of the Prince's Council in Bahrain, and getting into his office was tougher, and more interesting, than getting in the Oval Office. Security seemed much tighter in Bahrain and the buildings more elaborate. I had the opportunity to meet with former British Prime Minister Tony Blair, and he was a very interesting guy. Finally, and this will sound silly, but it's true— you can ask my wife—the Queen of England waved to me at the Kentucky Derby!

So, those are some of the high points of dozens of trips I have taken to Washington, D.C., and some meetings with global officials, since that lunch in Seoul. So, what did I learn?

In my home country, the United States, unfortunately, the more contact I have with people from all political perspectives, the more I have become convinced that politics is a team sport at the expense of our country. It frustrates me when my conservative friends demean the Democrats, and I am equally frustrated when my liberal friends talk about conservatives like they are cold-hearted.

I have spent time with plenty of people in both camps and am convinced that the demonization of people and parties with which you disagree is harmful. However, we want to root for our "team," and this will upset some people, but while the blind loyalty we give those who represent our team may be the "easy button," it is also lazy and unproductive. And both sides are equally guilty.

I saw this at a distance during the Bush 43 years when it seemed like the Democrats did not like him and whatever he proposed was going to be challenged by them. They did not want to give him a win. I saw the other side of this personally during the Obama years.

One of the times I was invited to the Obama White House was for a meeting to discuss our nation's infrastructure, which is deteriorating at a fast pace. Based on global benchmarks, the U.S. is falling way behind in infrastructure investment, and long-term, this will give other countries that are actually investing in infrastructure a significant economic advantage. Treasury Secretary Jack Lew was in the meeting, and we discussed the Obama Administration's strong desire to make infrastructure investments. When I would visit Capitol Hill and talk to Republicans, they all recognized the problem, and Republican presidential candidates would complain about what a shame it is that we are not investing in infrastructure. But from my view, the Republicans could not work with President Obama on this issue because they did not want to give him a "win." The country was taking second place to team.

During the Obama Administration, I served on the Manufacturing Council, a group of about twenty-five business leaders who advised the Secretary of Commerce. As Co-Chair of the Tax and Trade Committee, I worked on several issues, including the repatriation of profits U.S. companies were keeping overseas because of the high taxes due when bringing those dollars back to the U.S. The short explanation of this problem is that when U.S. companies make profits overseas, they do not pay U.S. taxes on those profits until they bring them back to the U.S. So if the U.S. tax rate is high on those profits, the company will just keep the money overseas.

Our Committee met with White House staff and strongly recommended that the tax rates be adjusted so that money could be brought to the U.S. for investment, where many of the companies wanted to bring the money anyway. The Obama tax team fully agreed and proposed a repatriation rate of 14 percent but could not get the Republican Congress to consider it. Again, Republicans I met with on Capitol Hill were supportive of the plan but could not do anything that seemed to give President Obama a win even though pretty much everyone agreed it was the right thing to do. However, the Republicans did support the repatriation tax rate change after President Trump came into office, and it was adjusted to 15.5 percent.

I don't want to beat up on just Republicans because this is an equally big problem for both parties. To be crystal clear, these are just examples that I lived through personally, but this is an equal problem for both Democrats and Republicans. And, interestingly, people in both parties see this problem as obvious in the other party but not in their own. Talk about self-deception.

There is a tremendous amount on which both sides agree. We could make a lot of positive progress for our country if we were not afraid of the other team appearing to get a win. In my opinion, this fear of the other team seeming to win is unpatriotic.

I understand the importance of values to which the parties prescribe, but just because others may have a different worldview does not mean everything they say is wrong. We could make tremendous progress as a nation if our leaders would look beyond their team and do what is best for our country.

Reflections

- Often, politicians are more concerned about their teams (i.e., parties) than what is best for the country.
- This is a problem of both political parties.

- There is a lot of common ground to make progress if politicians would put country first.

Chapter 6

Faith

Do you ever feel like the world is a scary place? I do.

Can we fix this? By loving others and appreciating those different from us.

How can we love those we fear? Life makes more sense with an eternal perspective.

Can we actually be a better person because of going through hard times? Definitely.

Over the years, I have visited many religious facilities, including Shinto temples in Japan, Hindu temples in Thailand, a Buddhist temple in Cambodia, the Vatican, and other Christian churches all around the world, and to, but not in, Muslim mosques in the Middle East.

I have discussed faith with people all over the world who worship differently than I do. In Kuala Lumper, Malaysia, I have become friends with a Muslim who converted from Christianity, and it is interesting to hear his journey. In Jerusalem, I spoke with an agnostic Jew who identifies as Jewish culturally but cannot be sure there really is a God. In Barbados, our tour guide was a seeker who was highly interested in learning about Christianity, and before our day was over, he professed his faith in Christ. In Cuba, I enjoyed visiting the beautiful Havana Cathedral, and I appreciated hearing how Catholics there expressed faith while under an authoritarian regime. These experiences, and many more like them, have helped me better understand others, and as a Christian, they have helped as I have tried to live up to Jesus's clear direction to love others. And loving others means even those who do not look like us or think like us, even people who hate us.

The one thing I have noticed at all these places of worship, and in my conversations around the globe about faith with all kinds of people, is a deep sincerity and a longing to find God. Get the learner in you ready for a look at Christianity and the experiences I've had that have helped define my faith over the years.

Why Do Many Not See Christianity as Irresistible?

Many people, including Christians, get confused about the rules laid out in the Old Testament. Often, people will pick a verse, usually out of context, to build a strong position against some practice or other group. Or they will take an Old Testament mindset heavily based on rules, and frequently, it makes non-Christians view Christ followers as hateful or angry.

I grew up in a legalistic Christian church and school environment that was really (I mean REALLY) strict. There were all kinds of rules related to music, how long my hair could be, and what movies I could watch (oh, wait, I could not watch ANY movies). For a while, the girls at our church and Christian school wore no pants, only dresses. As a teen, I remember visiting a water park and all the girls wore dresses over their knee-length shorts as they were going down the water slides (bet we were really enticing converts when they saw that). Our leaders loved us and were well-intentioned, and despite the rules, those were wonderful days with lots of great friends. I know part of the person I am today is a result of that time.

Thankfully, our church transitioned out of that legalistic thinking a long time ago, and after my dad died in 1998, I set out on a quest to understand apologetics so that I could know what I believed and why I believed it. I was on a search for truth, and that search deepened my Christian faith.

What we often forget, or ignore, is that the New Testament clearly states that Old Testament law does not apply to us today. I am not a theologian, but for a good perspective on this, read Andy Stanley's book *Irresistible*.

Explorations in Faith

In the rest of this chapter, I want to look at faith and religion as I have experienced it throughout the world. Traveling has presented me with many opportunities to deepen my faith as a Christian while simultaneously learning about other faiths.

1,000-Year-Old Eggs

Speaking to students at Taiwan's National Taipei University on a hot December night in a room with broken air conditioning was an interesting experience. The students had come to hear an American CEO talk about global trends so they could better understand how to prepare for a future that was dramatically changing. I love talking about global trends, and despite being brutally hot in the room, it was a fun presentation, and I appreciated the students' interest.

After the presentation, my host, whom I had met a year before in Malaysia and was the Director of International Affairs at the University, took me, some of Taipei's industry leaders, and a couple of students to a fancy restaurant where I first tried a 1,000-year-old egg. The dinner was nice, the food was good, the company was pleasant, the conversation was interesting, and as always, I enjoyed being with people who had a different life perspective than me. As we were finishing dinner, my host asked if I would like to join the group as they went to worship at a nearby temple.

After agreeing to tag along, we walked through the backstreets of Taipei's most historic district until coming upon the beautiful Longshan Temple. Longshan Temple is over 300 years old and is now a multi-deity center used by people of Taoist, Buddhist, and Confucian faiths. Not knowing the protocol, especially with three faiths worshiping in one temple, I was careful not to do anything that would be disrespectful or embarrass my guests.

Most people are familiar with Buddhism and Confucianism. The other faith worshipped at the temple, Taoism, is a multi-deity, even pantheistic religion, so there was a lot going on at the temple from a faith perspective. Frankly, as a Christian, I was a little nervous about whether I should even go to the temple, but I have a high sense of curiosity, and seeing how other people worship was an interesting experience.

Faith in Kuwait

Visiting Kuwait felt almost surreal. As the focal point of the first Gulf War and its aftermath, Kuwait had been in the news for most of the twenty years before my visit. While the country was largely rebuilt, there are places intentionally left as they were immediately after the war to remind both Kuwaitis and visitors to the country alike of the Iraqi invasion. A country that is a short drive to Iran and smaller than New Jersey, while sharing borders with both Iraq and Saudi Arabia, Kuwait is in the middle of what some consider the world's most dangerous region. However, I felt totally safe on my visit, and my hosts did an outstanding job of not only making me comfortable but helping me see the business opportunity in the country.

Kuwait is one of the world's most conservative Muslim countries, so I was not surprised when one afternoon, as we were driving back from a new real estate project under construction near the Saudi border, my host asked me if we could stop at a local mosque so he could participate in the afternoon prayers. Of course, I did not object. I had been to mosques before, including the magnificent Blue Mosque in Istanbul, Turkey, that shares property with the Hagia Sophia near the important Bosphorus Strait, but nothing quite like this. This mosque is in the middle of the desert with not much around. It was all highway, and the mosque we were visiting must have been built for the exact purpose my host was using it, to not miss prayer while travelling. We pulled into the mosque parking lot, and he found a spot just a few feet from the front door and left me in the car while he went in to pray. I admired his commitment.

After he got back in the car, his first words were, "So, you must be a Christian?" I was a little taken back because Kuwait is such a conservative Muslim country, but we ended up spending an hour just a few feet from that mosque sharing our respective faiths with each other. We shared life experiences and discovered a lot of similarities. Both of us love our families, faith, and countries without being militant. Neither of us converted the other, but it was one of the most interesting and intellectually stimulating discussions I have ever experienced.

This was truly one of those situations where being a learner— being open to perspectives other than my own—gave me the opportunity to explore my faith in ways I wouldn't have considered before the conversation.

Walking on Water

My first trip to Israel was dreamlike. As the plane was descending toward Tel Aviv, I found myself looking out the window in awe at a place with so much world history and, more important to me, the land where much of the Bible was played out. Both times I visited Israel were for business purposes, but in each case, I tried to spend time taking in as much of the country as possible. There is so much history in Israel that it is hard to drive more than a few miles without a historical landmark. Driving from the coast to the Sea of Galilee, we passed Mt. Carmel and also Nazareth, where Jesus grew up.

While at the Sea of Galilee, I was thrilled to be able to wake skate (think wakeboard without the boots) behind one of our company's boats. We took off from Tiberius on a beautiful day and drove the boat north toward Capernaum, near where Jesus walked on water. The sea was a little bumpy that day, but I wasn't going to miss this chance, so I wake skated while imagining what it was like when Jesus walked on the same water 2,000 years ago. After ending my ride and floating in the sea waiting for the boat to come back and pick me up, I was on a spiritual high thinking of Jesus walking on and fishing in the same sea where I was floating.

Later, while driving to the city of Eilat, on the southern coast of Israel, it seemed like we were passing one place of biblical significance after another. We also drove through Palestinian areas, and I knew that there was a lot of suffering behind the very high fences that protected the highway from people who might throw something at a passing vehicle out of frustration.

Eilat itself was interesting, and the boat demo we did there was on part of the Red Sea where Egypt, Israel, Jordan, and Saudi Arabia all come together. On the boat, we could see all four countries at the same time, which was fascinating and a little scary. Not long before my visit, a terrorist rocket had been shot from the Sinai Peninsula into Eilat.

On my second trip to Israel, I took a day off to spend walking the streets of Jerusalem. I walked through all four quarters of Jerusalem (Christian, Jewish, Muslim, and Armenian) and was impressed with how easy it was to walk from one quarter to another and how well everyone seemed to get along. Of course, I walked the Via Dolorosa and visited all the popular sites like the Church of the Holy Sepulchre and the Wailing Wall where I was honored to put my written prayer in the cracks of the Wall as had so many before me.

The first thing most people ask me about Israel is whether visiting there is safe. On both of my trips, I felt totally safe. There is always plenty of military personnel around reminding visitors that it is a dangerous region, but I never felt threatened or insecure. Even the disputed Golan Heights area, where I went to visit a wakeboard school, felt safe. Maybe it was a false sense of security, but I felt safe enough to happily support my daughter Amanda spending ten days touring Israel after my two trips to the country.

No trip to Israel is complete without spending time on the Mount of Olives. There, I visited the Garden of Gethsemane and especially enjoyed the view of Jerusalem. Overlooking the Dome of the Rock and historic Jerusalem from the Mount of Olives was possibly my most impactful experience in Israel, second only to touching the earth through the floor in the Church of the Holy Sepulchre on the spot where many people believe Jesus was crucified. On top of the Mount of Olives is the Chapel of the Ascension, where many people believe Jesus ascended after his resurrection. Realizing that the most important moments in biblical history happened within the view I was enjoying significantly impacted me. The Bible was coming alive.

The World of Faith

Over the years, I have heard people say they wish God would be more revealing. The problem with insisting God reveal Himself is that it ignores what we know pleases God: faith. Most people think that God has all these rules we must follow to please Him, but that is not what we are taught in the book of Hebrews where it clearly says it is impossible to please God without being good. Actually, that is not what the book of Hebrews says—it states that it is impossible to please God without faith. I have no idea why it is faith that pleases God, and it is not necessary for me to know. I am just happy that He tells us what pleases Him.

Since we know that it is faith that pleases God, it seems obvious that He gives us just enough information to require a Faith Leap. This Faith Leap is where many people struggle. We want proof. The interesting thing is that if we really study the information we have, the Faith Leap is probably much easier than many people think. I know this is true from personal experience.

After my dad's death, I spent a lot of time studying apologetics (defense of the scripture or, as I viewed it, proof that what the Bible says is true). There is a ton of proof that the Bible is true, but unfortunately, most people don't want to search for it. They want easy proof that does not require faith.

I have had the opportunity to speak at churches in Africa, the Caribbean, and Central America where people are making huge sacrifices to worship and live out their faith. In places like Ethiopia, Kenya, Haiti, and Guatemala, I have seen people who have virtually nothing make sacrifices to live out their faith and support their spiritual community. Frankly, it forces me to realize how much stronger they are than me and how much more committed.

I feel persecuted if my air conditioner goes out or if a business deal goes sideways, which is crazy because I have seen people counting their blessings who have much less than me. Sometimes, we consider blessings a new car or a raise of pay, but that is not how Jesus described blessings in Matthew 5 during his Sermon on the Mount.

I want to talk about why I think so many peoples' faith is waning and how we can learn to live our best lives by honoring God.

We Are Distracted

Speaking at a church in Kenya on a beautiful Sunday morning, I was impressed with how many people walked long distances to worship. They didn't have cars to take them, and they certainly were not walking that far to hear me, or they would be greatly disappointed. They sacrificed because they strongly believed in their God, Jesus, and wanted to honor him by gathering with other believers. If this is obvious to the people I have seen in Kenya, or Pignon, Haiti, Guatemala City, and the many other places around the world where I have seen Christians sacrificing for their faith, why would it not be so obvious to others?

Honestly, I think sometimes Christians distract others and hurt the cause we are supposed to be representing. The New Testament is very clear that to be a Christian, a person must do one thing: believe in Jesus. Jesus himself said that in the Bible's most well-known verse, John 3:16. The New Testament does not say that to be a Christian, someone needs to be a Republican or Democrat, believe Jonah was swallowed by a whale or that creation happened in six days. The Bible does not say that only people with certain sexual preferences or who have never had an abortion are Christian. We Christians can get incredibly hung up on issues that don't determine where someone spends eternity and, honestly, I think there are two particular distractions that push away potential believers: science and politics.

Since earlier in this book I discuss politics, I won't belabor it again here, but it sure seems like many Christians push people away because of their idol, politics. I heard someone say that we will know that politics are our idol if we tend to view every situation as a matter of right vs. left or think the solution to our problems is to elect a certain party or person. If many Christians believed faith were the solution to the world's problems as much as they believe electing the right person is the solution, or if we were as enthusiastic about loving God and others as we are about elections, I believe the world would be a much better place. Unfortunately, in my opinion, many Christians' obsession with politics is repelling people from our faith, not bringing them to Jesus as Christians are told to do in the Great Commission.

Additionally, many Christians reflexively oppose current science, and it just makes them seem backwards and reduces their influence. This is especially true when Christians proclaim that science is just trying to debunk Christianity and make them look bad. Honestly, my experience is that most people of science are just searching for truth and don't revolve their world around trying to prove or disprove Christianity.

On my second trip to Alaska, I was surprised to see both the devastation of forests because of a beetle that is living longer in the age of global warming and the shrinking of Portage Glacier because of rising temperatures. Portage Glacier was especially impactful to me because of the photos that showed the minimal seasonal shrinkage of the glacier over several decades and the now aggressive shrinkage the past couple of decades.

And on a recent January business trip to Germany, I heard people asking, "What happened to our winters?" While the scientific and anecdotal evidence is overwhelming that the world is warming, some will use a particularly cold week as evidence that it is all made up, and for some reason, Christians seem to lead this effort. The question is why?

The same is the case with creation. Scientists use the expanding universe as evidence that the world started with a big bang. Based on the size of the universe and its rate of expansion, they estimate the Big Bang happened a little over 13 billion years ago. It seems to me we are debating timing. The Bible says that in the beginning, God created the heavens and the earth—maybe He did it with a big bang. That doesn't threaten my faith at all. I am not a scientist or a theologian, so I could be out-debated by either side on this; however, when we make the most important issue the timing of creation, which according to my reading of the New Testament is not a condition to a relationship with God, we neglect doing what Jesus said was most important.

It feels good to feel right. Feelings are powerful. However, chasing that feeling of rightness can be a trap that keeps others from experiencing a relationship with God.

The Absolute Best

My dad, also Bill Yeargin, was the best man I have ever known. I had a front-row seat to view his life, and he never let me or anyone down. He worked hard, often two jobs, took us to church, coached my sports teams, and NEVER missed any event (even practices) of which I was part. His integrity and faith were unparalleled. He was the type of guy who would go back to the store if he found out he was given too much change. At church, he was a deacon, teacher, bus driver and on and on—he did everything. He was the kind of friend you could count on, and he spent thousands of hours investing in the lives of young people through youth sports. I know almost everyone loves their dad, but mine was very special, and I was very blessed to have had him.

When Dad was diagnosed with Parkinson's disease in his late forties, it was tough on our family and led to a very challenging fifteen years for all of us, but especially him and Mom. Dad eventually went on disability, and Mom was an angel as she took care of him. My mom, brother Doug, Aunt Debbie, and I basically lived with dad in a hospice room the last few weeks of his life, and while his passing was a glorious release from suffering for him, it was tough on me. I never questioned my faith after Dad's death, but I did question why God would allow my dad to suffer and die. Dad was the best man I have ever known.

So why would God allow someone so good to get so sick and suffer horribly for years before dying?

I struggled with this for a while, but about three years after dad died, I had an experience that significantly impacted my view of Dad's death. One of my previous books (*What Would Dad Say?*) is about this experience, so I will just summarize it here.

After dad passed, it was about three years before I had the opportunity to travel back to the cemetery in Oxford, North Carolina, where he is buried. When I finally did, I was on a business trip and only had a small amount of time; however, I went to visit Dad's grave and found myself engulfed in a highly emotional experience.

As I stood at the grave, I was overtaken by the fact that while Dad's body was in that grave, he was now in heaven and had an eternal perspective. Even though I had grown up in church and heard people talk before about developing an eternal perspective, that day at Dad's grave was the first time I have ever really gotten my mind around that concept (to the extent I can). I began to realize that life is like a grain of sand on the beach compared to eternity and that we should be focused on the eternal perspective and not our short time on earth.

I still was sorry that Dad suffered, but I also realized that in light of his now-eternal perspective, it did not seem as bad. I also knew that Dad, now in heaven, would not change anything! He had been used according to God's plan, and lives had been changed and people had become Christians as a result of what he went through. Even today, years later, people are blessed by the book that was written because of his suffering.

Beginning to think more about having an eternal perspective was one of the most (if not *the* most) significant paradigm shifts in my life. The idea expanded well beyond Dad's death to all aspects of my life. I started to wonder often if what I was doing mattered in light of eternity.

I also decided to continue making sure I was rock-solid in what I believed about God.

Our Role as Christians

While visiting both Cambodia and Uganda, I received an up-close view of how extremely devastating genocide is to a country and its people. In both places, it is a stark observation to realize that there is an entire generation of people missing. In both countries, the genocide eventually ended, but in Cambodia, it gave way to a horrible period of sex trafficking young girls. Living through all of that could easily make one wonder, "Why am I here, what is my role?"

Even those who have not lived in such dire circumstances have gone through life wondering, "What is my role in the world?" Feeling like we matter and have significance are normal human desires. Fortunately for us, the Bible is very clear on our roles: We just have to be willing to read it.

However, reading through the Bible can be daunting, especially if you start with the Old Testament, which can be tough to understand. But if the reader is up for it, the Old Testament has a recurring theme: Follow God's commands, and blessings will follow.

In between the Old and New Testaments, in what is sometimes called the inter-testament period, a lot happened. Alexander the Great came through the area and claimed it for his own. After Alexander died, the Greeks tried to Hellenize the area and the Jews revolted, which eventually led to the Roman takeover. During this time, a group called the Pharisees formed and became influential religious leaders who ushered in an era of legalism.

It was during this era that Jesus was born, and everyone embraced him, right? Nope, everyone did not embrace him. Actually, the religious leaders of the time, the above-mentioned Pharisees, did not like Jesus. He threatened the Pharisees' privilege, and they tried to trick him into making a mistake so they could kill him.

It was during one of the times the Pharisees were trying to trick Jesus that we learn exactly what our role is, without ambiguity. One of their Pharisee lawyers asked Jesus a trick question. He asked him what the most important commandment is. The story can be read in Matthew 22, but basically, Jesus said to love God and others. In some versions, it can be read that Jesus said loving others is equally important to loving God.

Love God and others... sounds simple, huh? The difficult part of this formula for me was the loving God part. How do you do that? Follow rules, go to church, have a bumper sticker on my car?

As I dug into this, I realized that Jesus makes it very clear that we love God by loving others. He shared this same point with Peter when he told him to "feed my sheep" and again in Matthew 25 when he said that whatever we do for "the least of these" we do for him. Love others, that's our role.

Resurrection Changes Everything

There is debate about whether the Chapel of the Ascension on the Mount of Olives, which I mentioned earlier, is the actual place where Jesus ascended, but as a Christian, there can be no debate about whether Jesus was resurrected and its importance to Christianity. In fact, the apostle Paul, who most people believe was martyred for his faith, said in his letter to the people of Corinth that without the resurrection of Jesus, our Christian faith is in vain and that we should be pitied.

So, I took a close look at the most important issue in the Bible, the single issue upon which our faith hangs: the resurrection. This is a tough one because you cannot prove what is not there; the body is gone. However, after my dad's death, as I studied the resurrection, it became impossible for me to believe that it did not happen. As an example, this is some of what I found:

- **It is in the Bible**: The resurrection is recorded in the Gospels and the rest of the New Testament. It is interesting how we have lots of books from antiquity that do not have their authenticity questioned, but for some reason, the Bible is questioned. The Bible, in different parts written by different authors, clearly records the resurrection.
- **Eyewitnesses**: There were over 500 eyewitnesses to Jesus being alive after His obvious death. There is no other event in history with 500 eyewitnesses that is questioned.

- **Changed lives**: After the death of Jesus, His followers were cowering and in hiding, afraid that they too would be killed. Something clearly happened that totally changed their lives. They did a complete 180-degree change and went from hiding in seclusion to risking their lives by boldly preaching the story of Jesus on the streets. A resurrection would inspire such a dramatic change.

- **The martyred lives**: History records that elevent of the twelve apostles were martyred for their faith. If they had made up the story of Jesus' resurrection, it seems like the lies would have stopped when the killing started. However, the resurrection was so powerful in their lives that they were willing to die horrible deaths for their faith

- **Secular historians**: The historians of the time recorded happenings in Jerusalem and changed lives completely consistently with the Bible.

- **Scrutiny**: Many, many people have tried to prove the resurrection did not happen, and while there is not one instance of someone proving it did not happen, there are innumerable stories of people who were trying to discredit Christianity themselves coming to faith in Jesus.

The above information on the resurrection is just an example of what I learned during my searching after Dad's death. I am certainly not a theologian or apologist, but I do know there is plenty of proof regarding the resurrection. If Jesus really did rise from the dead, I couldn't ignore that. It deserved a response from me and solidified my faith.

I am often asked why God does not reveal himself more obviously. Someone will say that they would believe if God would be more real to them, show them He is real through an appearance of some type, say, sky writing or showing up in their living room. Momentarily ignoring the fact that God did appear as a person in

Jesus, I believe there is a good reason why He does not appear in the way many people would like Him to do. God wants us to have faith; according to the New Testament's book of Hebrews, it is what pleases Him.

Reflections

- There is plenty of evidence to be a Christian.

- Life makes more sense with an eternal perspective.

- Christians can cause their own obstacles. Politics, science and legalism are examples.

- Our role is to love God and love others.

- We love God by loving others.

- Faith pleases God.

Chapter 7

Around the World in 26 Pages

Like most people, I easily fall into a trap of thinking I know a lot about someone I have never met or someplace I have never been. Innumerable times, I have had my perspective shifted by meeting someone or seeing a place firsthand. The people you meet, the things you see, the smells, sounds, and touch of other places are hard to appreciate without personal experience. I have never visited a place without leaving a different person. Visiting the world will change you.

This would be a long book if I tried to share every experience and every time I was "educated" by visiting somewhere new, but I can still share some of my favorite moments. This chapter is a quick "around the world" perspective of some of the places that had the biggest impact on me and my thinking.

Africa

Africa is extremely complex. It is a diverse continent with a rich history, and while it may be the world's richest continent from a resource perspective, it has the world's poorest people. The past 200 years have been tumultuous for Africa with colonization, slavery, independence, a tough post-colonial transition, the Cold War, and now a slow, steady path toward democracy and stability. Because of its resources, Africa has been viewed as extremely valuable to both countries and companies, but unfortunately, few of the benefits of those resources have reached the African people. I have travelled to Africa on several occasions and have spent time in Morocco, Egypt, Ethiopia, Uganda, Kenya, South Africa, and Namibia. I have seen both the struggle and opportunities firsthand and believe Africa has tremendous potential.

Africa has market potential today and will become a significant market force in the years ahead. Many agree with this, and over the past several years, the buzz phrase (and philosophy) of "trade, not aid" has been largely adopted by governments and philanthropic organizations around the world. There does not seem to be much argument over the strategy, but challenges arise when we try to execute the strategy and minimize unintended consequences.

So, why is Africa so strategically important?

First, Africa has over a billion people. We should do everything possible to help them develop strong markets that benefit the people of Africa and help them become customers for U.S. products, including boats, of course. Over the last ten years, our company has sold a lot of boats to Africa, but we know the market could be significantly larger. If done right, we can develop healthy markets and trade with over a billion people, which will make their lives much better and allow them to enjoy many of the things much of the world takes for granted.

The second reason relates to a strategic global concern. For nearly twenty years, China has taken a strategic approach to Africa, investing heavily in an effort to tie up the continent's resources for the decades ahead. I have personally seen ports, highways, government buildings, airports, and sports stadiums China has built in Africa to gain favor with the African people and obtain the rights to the resources of their countries. China now can block access to key resources needed by the world economy. This could seriously impact the global economy in the years ahead and even become a serious national defense concern.

Africa is an exciting place full of opportunity. On each of my visits, I have felt and seen that opportunity firsthand. My first of several visits to Africa was with Wayne Huizenga on the trip to South Africa I previously wrote about. Wayne's house overlooked

Kruger National Park, separated only by a river that wild game would visit for water each evening.

Safaris in South Africa are exciting, and I've had the opportunity to do several. Probably the most exciting safari moment for me was in the outside seat of an open-air Jeep when a cheetah we were viewing got up and started walking directly toward us. The guides in the Jeep said to stay very, very still, and believe me, that was hard to do. The cheetah walked to us and ran its body alongside the jeep to scratch itself like you might see a pet cat do on a chair. Sitting in the outside seat of the Jeep, I was literally six inches from the cheetah; I could have easily reached out my hand and scratched its back, but of course, I didn't.

During one Africa trip, I took a walking safari where we drove to the middle of the preserve before getting out of the Jeep and walking. It sounds fun, and it was, but I am sure my blood pressure was setting new highs—it was a bit scary. Each of us on the walking safari had a guide with a gun, but thankfully, the weapons were not needed. Interestingly, my guide told me that the deadliest animal in Africa is the hippopotamus, which runs over anything between it and the water. The whole time we were walking, I was thinking the guide's weapon would not be much use against a charging hippo.

My highest safari recommendation for those going to Africa is to do one at night. My night safari was in the Shamwari Game Reserve, and it was spectacular. During the day, you really have no idea how much wildlife surrounds you, but at night when the guide shines a floodlight into the savanna, you see literally thousands of eyes.

Those who want to see African wildlife without going into a reserve should visit **Namibia**. Flying into Windhoek, Namibia, with about a two-hour drive to my meeting, the road was surrounded by wildlife. On some stretches of highway, it felt like driving through a tourist attraction. Almost everything that can be seen in African game reserves can be seen on the highway in Namibia, though I did not see a lion while driving or stopping, thankfully.

Further north, **Uganda** and **Kenya** are both fun places to visit. While there, it is impossible to miss the poverty but also to feel the potential. People in these countries are well aware of the wealth differences between them and much of the world and want to see their countries develop. One of the reasons I am bullish on Africa is not only because of their immense resources but also because of their smart and talented people who are generally curious and have a strong desire to be learners. Given an opportunity, they can thrive.

When visiting **Ethiopia**, I expected to see the worst poverty I had observed. I was surprised when boarding and then travelling to the country on Ethiopian Airlines out of Washington, D.C., as I realized this was one of the nicest planes and best air service I had experienced. Landing in Ethiopia's capital, Addis Ababa, the city seemed like any other capital city I'd visited on the continent. But, as I wrote about in the service trips chapter, a couple hours outside of Addis Ababa, it was like nothing had changed in 2,000 years.

Saharan Africa felt totally different than Sub-Saharan Africa, and I was able to experience the region in both Egypt and Morocco.

Visiting **Egypt** after meetings in Europe, and shortly after the Egyptian revolution, brought its own set of concerns. I arrived in Cairo unaware my host had arranged for me to bypass the normal customs and immigration process. Not knowing this, walking to the bottom of the deplaning stairs, I was surprised to see a man holding a sign with my name on it next to a car. Since I was the only one deplaning getting this treatment, I figured it was either really good or really bad—thankfully, it ended up being really good. The man told me to get in the car, and I complied. The car took me to an immigration and customs office unlike any I had ever seen. It was luxurious, and I was the only passenger in the office. After a quick look at my passport, one of the officers told me to have a nice visit, and I walked out into an area where my host was waiting.

I have already written about the scariest part of my Egypt visit, but most of my time there was fun and exciting. Meals by the Nile River, time spent in high-energy markets, and of course, the absolute must-see Egyptian site: the pyramids and sphinx at Giza, just outside Cairo. Despite my scary experience, Egypt is a cultural and historical site like few others, and I would highly recommend it. I hope to go back someday myself.

Morocco was like Egypt but a little friendlier and with a unique Moroccan flair. I loved walking through the Moroccan markets and brought home a unique hand-made silver tea set. And, of course, as most American tourists do, I visited Rick's Café, made famous by Humphrey Bogart and Ingrid Bergman in the movie *Casablanca*. The movie was made on a Warner Brothers set in Burbank, California, so the café is not actually from the movie, but the owners do a great job of recreating the look and feel while also serving great food.

Africa has had a lot of struggles, and if you want to understand it better, I highly recommend *The Looting Machine* by Tom Burgis. In his well-written book, Burgis explains the way Africans have been exploited and offers suggestions to fix the problem. Despite the challenges, there is plenty of reason to believe that we may soon be entering the African century. I continue to be bullish on Africa and am excited that Africans have a bright future.

Asia

For a U.S. resident visiting Asia for the first time, it can be an awakening. The cities are so new, modern, luxurious, and energetic, they can make many U.S. cities seem old-fashioned and quaint. While Asia still has plenty of poor areas, visiting the most popular cities on the continent clearly demonstrates the wealth that has been generated in an area that not long ago was poor and trying to recover from WWII. It is hard to imagine that so much wealth could be generated so fast and how an entire continent could be largely transformed.

My first trip to Asia was in the late 1990s with my daughter Erin, who at the time was about eight years old. Getting in the taxi at Tokyo's Narita airport, Erin immediately fell asleep with her head on my lap. Exhausted from the long flight from the U.S., I too wanted to sleep in the cab but decided that I better stay awake as the taxi took us to our hotel directly across the street from the Imperial Palace. I was speaking at an event connected with the Tokyo Boat Show, but Erin and I also managed to find some time to tour Tokyo, **Japan**.

One of our days in Tokyo Erin and I spent with my best friend from high school, Rob, who had moved there after college. Rob gave a local's view of Tokyo, which included dinner at one of his favorite restaurants which we enjoyed sitting on the floor. We walked around Tokyo enjoying both the tourist sites and local haunts. It was a great adventure with Erin that I will forever treasure.

Since that first trip to Japan with Erin, I have been back to Japan several times and have always loved it there. I can understand why Rob would be attracted to the country he now calls home. Our company owns a bass fishing boat manufacturer, and bass fishing is very popular in Japan. On one trip, the president of our bass fishing boat company and I fished on Lake Biwa with a boatload (literally) of paparazzi following us to capture our every move and the fish we caught. The same group of photographers followed us into a bass fishing store, and the next week our distributor sent us newspapers and magazines of the American bass fishing executives, us, in Japan.

The hardest part of that trip for me was staying awake at a dinner we hosted one night there when the jet lag kicked in big time. I was drinking anything that had caffeine in it and was literally physically struggling to stay awake at the table. It was an interesting and fun crowd who were sharing stories of fishing in Japan, but the jet lag that night was more than I could fight.

Our family spent a week in Kyoto one summer; it is a special place. The Shinto temples, Imperial Palace, and bamboo forests in and around Kyoto, combined with the quaintness of a town that is fun to walk, makes Kyoto a place people love to visit.

My daughter Amanda and I visited Hiroshima, a place that will change anyone who visits. Seeing firsthand the effect of the first atomic bomb used in war was impactful. It is hard to believe that one bomb, which is tiny compared to the bombs global powers possess today, could cause so much damage and kill so many people. The atomic dome, mass burial site, and atomic bomb museum with pictures and stories of the carnage are hard to visit without shaping your thinking about the world. If nothing else, it makes it clear that the world should work hard to ensure we never use one of those weapons again.

My first visit to Seoul, **South Korea**, was fun because my hotel was in the city just a short walk from a market selling all kinds of interesting food. I was surprised to learn how much boating is done on the Han River that runs through Seoul. On one later trip, an approaching typhoon ran me and our team out of South Korea while we were having a wakeboarding event in the country, which resulted in my first trip upstairs in a Boeing 747; our team was alone up there and had a good time.

Singapore is another must-visit place when travelling to Asia. The city/country feels very western and is impeccably clean and pretty. Amanda joined me on one visit to Singapore, and while visiting the world-famous Raffles Hotel we found it interesting to see ATM machines that paid out gold bars.

Leaving **Thailand's** Suvarnabhumi Airport in a taxi, heading toward downtown Bangkok, I was surprised to see a plethora of billboards advertising medical procedures. Pretty much any procedure a patient would need was advertised like lawyers, car dealers, or vasectomies in Florida. Speaking to my host there, I learned that medical tourism in Thailand is a big business with world-class health care. Patients can fly to the country first class, stay in luxurious hospitals, and get great medical care for a fraction of the cost of the procedure in their home country—and particularly the U.S. I thought it was a good place to get some plastic surgery done that would give me a more youthful look, but since I only had a couple days there, it didn't work out. Just as well, I don't think my family would have considered it funny if I came home looking different.

Bangkok is a bustling, friendly town with pictures of their king proudly shown off around the city. My hotel was walking distance from the Erawan Shrine which is home of the famous four-face Buddha that is actually not Buddha—or Buddhist at all. The four-faced Buddha is actually a Hindu shrine featuring the Hindu trinity including Lord Brahma, Lord Vishnu the sustainer, and Lord Siva the destroyer. Regardless of the misnomer, it was still an interesting place to visit and was a popular place for people from Bangkok to pray.

In every country, there are interesting cultural differences, and Thailand was no different. In Thailand, it is perfectly acceptable to pick your nose in public but considered bad etiquette to not completely cover your mouth when using a toothpick. Seeing different norms around the world is one of the exciting and educational parts of travel.

China is an amazing country, and like the United States, it has many different aspects. However, my first visits to China were to areas where many of the residents don't even consider themselves as part of China: Honk Kong and Macau.

There are few cities in the world with the vibrancy of Hong Kong. The electricity of an economic powerhouse with residents showing off their yachts, fancy sports cars, and expensive suits combined with dragon boats on the harbor displaying the charms of an earlier time make Hong Kong one of the most exciting cities in the world to visit. Even the plethora of skyscrapers in Hong Kong have unique holes in the middle of them that almost all first-time visitors wonder about. They allow dragons travelling from the mountains to the sea easy passage through the building, which the people of Hong Kong believe adds positive energy to the building. It's some very expensive feng shui.

Hong Kong was under British control until 1997 when the United Kingdom gave up control of the island, turning it over to China. As part of the agreement to turn Hong Kong over, China agreed to leave the Hong Kong economic system alone until 2047, though some argue that China is already reneging on that promise.

Visiting Victoria Peak in Hong Kong at night is one of the most spectacular city views in the world and possibly the globe's best place to take a city-view selfie. I have a photo of my daughter Amanda and I taken on a clear night that is one of my all-time favorite pictures.

Not far from Hong Kong is *Macau*, the Las Vegas of Asia. The two cities have some of the same casinos and gambling opportunities, except that Macau takes in about five times the gambling dollars of Las Vegas. However, Macau is a place to go for serious gambling, while Las Vegas is focused more on entertainment. I have only been to Macau once, but for my money, Las Vegas is more fun to visit. However, getting to Macau can be fun; even if you are not up for spending the money for the helicopter ride many people take to get there, the high-speed ferry is an enjoyable experience.

Beijing, the capital of China, is also a fun place to visit unless you are there when they shut down the city because of pollution, which is often. I have been lucky, and my visits have been on low-pollution days, but I have heard stories of days when your eyes burn, schools and businesses are closed, traffic is limited, and the city grinds to a halt. The pollution in China is largely driven by numerous coal-fueled plants, and to China's credit, they are trying to move away from this form of energy.

Visiting Beijing isn't complete without spending time in Tiananmen Square, the Forbidden City, and the Olympic Park with its unique Aquatic Cube. And just an hour outside of Beijing is the Great Wall, which is, of course, the quintessential Chinese tourist spot. On one trip touring the Great Wall, some locals asked if they could take a picture with Amanda, my daughter. Amanda agreed, and it set off a chain reaction of people lining up to get their picture taken with her. At six-foot-one and non-Asian-looking, I stood out a fair bit myself, but no one was asking for my picture, at least not that day.

Flying into Wuhan, before it became famous for COVID-19, was an interesting experience. My meeting was actually about two hours outside of town, and driving through the Chinese country-side was eerie as we drove past some of China's infamous ghost cities. During the ride, I saw empty factory after empty factory, all of which had been built in anticipation of future economic growth. And to make it just a little more eerie, near each factory there were high-rise apartment buildings that were also standing empty, waiting for the employees who would eventually work in the factories. The Chinese were definitely expecting a lot of future growth and were prepared for it early. I wondered about the future impact on the Chinese economy when all the construction crews who were building these factories and apartments ran out of stuff to build and had nothing to do. I guess they would be the ones working in the new factories.

Arriving at the village about two hours outside Wuhan, the hotel was brand-new, and best I could tell, my travelling companion and I were some of their very first guests. The employees looked at us skeptically, and I found it interesting that they would not let us check out until someone was sent up to inspect our rooms for damage. I have stayed in innumerable hotels all over the world, but that is the only time someone has been sent up to check my room for damage before I could check out.

After checking out of the hotel and visiting a local factory for meetings, our Chinese host took us to a local restaurant, and my impression was that the eatery did not get many American guests. The food was good, and our hosts were gracious and friendly during the meal. As we were leaving, we passed a part of the restaurant that looked a bit like a shrine with several shelves of knick-knacks below a picture that appeared to have some significance I did not understand. The picture was slightly askew, and my travelling companion, one of our international sales reps, decided to straighten the picture. Big mistake: The picture fell off the hooks holding it on the wall and sent it crashing down on the shelves and knick-knacks, sending them into little pieces onto the floor. It was scary for a minute, but our hosts and the restaurant employees were very nice and even apologized as if they had made a mistake with the entire shrine. I was just thankful we did not get arrested.

India is an interesting country of vast extremes that I have had the opportunity to visit three times, one of which I wrote about in the service trip chapter.

Visiting the Taj Mahal in Agra was very interesting but not near as interesting as the scary four-hour drive to get there from New Delhi. People sometimes think New York City cab drivers are crazy drivers, but they are a grandma driving to church compared to the drivers in India. Think of the scariest car ride you can imagine, and multiply it exponentially. It was four hours of potholes, dirt roads, cows, pigs, and people walking in the road and no one honoring any type traffic laws or road courtesy. Drivers rode on whatever side of the road they wanted and often on the sidewalks; our driver was no exception.

Motorbikes seating families of five or six people were not uncommon. Our driver followed one motorbike with a family of five on it through their village and we were within ten feet of them, curving and winding through traffic and all kinds of other obstacles. I was one hundred percent sure we would run them over, but the driver just laughed off my concerns, and fortunately, we did not hit them. The villages along the way were poor, and I took pictures of them as I was passing through. It wasn't until months later when looking through the pictures that I realized in one village I had taken a picture of a young man defecating on the side of the road. The Taj Mahal was amazing, but it will always be the car ride there that brings back the keenest memories.

The Gateway to India in Mumbai was another fascinating site. Built in 1924, the eighty-three-foot-high monument was built to welcome King George on his visit to India with his wife, Queen Mary. The area surrounding the Gateway has a marketplace feel with vendors selling food and all kinds of other items. One walking vendor, who probably wasn't licensed or supposed to be there, was trying hard to sell me and one of our team athletes a pack of gigantic balloons. His demo balloon was huge, think the size of several nice size beach balls combined, and looked really cool. He wouldn't leave us alone, so after what we thought was some excellent street negotiating, we bought a pack of his balloons. We had only walked a few feet away before opening the package and realizing that he had sold us a package of much smaller balloons than he was showing us, but of course, he was long gone when we looked for him to complain. Lesson learned.

India is such a fascinating country, and it is always energizing to be there. On another trip, I was in an extremely poor slum and heard a group of people chanting and singing; it was a funeral procession, and the group was carrying the dead man on a bed of flowers up over their heads. I am not sure where they were taking him since I had not seen a cemetery anywhere around the slum, but it was interesting to see this ritual and how much they seemed to love and respect the dead gentleman.

I have been fortunate to visit other parts of Asia, but there is one more place I would be remiss not to mention: **Malaysia**. After three trips to Malaysia, it is one of my favorite places to visit. Kuala Lumpur is one of the world's most modern cities, and the surrounding areas are also very nice. The national government of Malaysia seems to have done a good job preparing for a post-oil economy, and the best part of Malaysia is that I have made some good friends there who I always enjoy seeing.

Australia

Australia is a beautiful and diverse country full of friendly people, among whom I have made many friends. I have always enjoyed going to Australia, but sometimes, I think I have flown twenty hours to land back in Florida. The weather, beaches, language, and palm trees are all familiar to Floridians travelling to the continent, but there are also plenty of unique aspects of the country to warrant a visit.

My first trip to Australia was about two weeks after 9/11, and I was with my daughter Amanda. We stopped in New Zealand for a couple days of fun before heading to Brisbane to speak at an industry conference. I was looking forward to the trip with Amanda, but travelling a couple weeks after 9/11 was a little spooky.

Boarding the plane in West Palm Beach, where I lived at the time, and later in Los Angeles to connect for our flight to Auckland, I found myself looking at every passenger on the plane and wondering if they could be a terrorist. I was actually playing through in my mind what I would do if someone jumped up and tried to commandeer the plane. I wasn't sure how I could stop them, but I knew I sure would try. The entire flight to Los Angeles, I was on high alert, and it wasn't until we were well on our way to Auckland that I could relax, mainly because I was just so tired. Being anxious is no fun.

New Zealand was as spectacular as anyone who has visited there would agree. The exchange rate was very favorable so Amanda and I could do pretty much anything we wanted at very little cost. We had dinner in the Auckland Tower at what was then a super-fancy restaurant with hors d'oeuvres, steaks, and dessert for less than $20 total, which even at the time would have been close to a $100 dinner in the U.S.

After visiting New Zealand, we travelled to Brisbane to spend a few days on the Gold Coast where I had the speaking engagement. We enjoyed our time there, and both Amanda and I were able to hold a koala, which was a highlight of the trip.

Sydney is a spectacular city best known for the iconic Sydney Opera House on the harbor. It is a fun and energetic city to walk around, and ferries take passengers into the harbor. The ferry to the seaside is particularly enjoyable because it leaves from the Sydney Opera House and takes passengers on a scenic path through the harbor to the town of Manly, a fun place with shops and restaurants near the beach. Brave visitors to Sydney should definitely climb to the top of the Sydney Harbor bridge, one of the most fun and exciting things to do in Australia with amazing views from the top.

My only trip to western Australia was a business trip to Perth. My main recollection of Perth was the miners who were passing through town to access the vast mines in northern Australia and the plain but highly expensive hotels resulting from having more miners visit than hotel rooms to accommodate them.

Middle East

I have written about the Middle East throughout this book and won't repeat that other than to say I have loved travelling there and always been treated well. **Abu Dhabi, Dubai, Bahrain, Kuwait,** and **Qatar** were particularly nice and modern. **Israel**, **Jordan,** and **Egypt** were culturally rich and inspiring.

Probably my most surprising visit was to **Turkey**, a country rich in history and full of surprises. **Istanbul**, formerly known as Constantinople, was the capital of both the Byzantine and Ottoman empires and is rich with history. The Blue Mosque, the Hagia Sophia, and the Bosphorus bridge which crosses the Bosphorus Strait from Europe to Asia are highlights, but the entire city is alive with energy of people bustling to interesting shops and markets— simply writing this makes me long to return. Leaving the city, I was not sure what to expect on the just over one-hour flight from Istanbul to Bodrum to meet one of our company's distributors, but within an hour of arriving, knew I was at a special place. Bodrum, Turkey, is spectacular with a castle, beautiful water, and impressive scenery—it is no wonder that many of the world's richest people vacation there.

Having been in some of the richest parts of the Middle East and some of the poorest parts, areas controlled by various sects, including Christians, Muslims, and Jews, and areas that are peaceful and areas that are war-torn, the one consistency is that the people want peace for their families. I understand the deep-rooted conflict that in some cases predates Jesus, but today, people want to know they can live in peace and their kids can go to school without fear and learn how to be more prosperous. I, like many people, have ideas about how that can be done, but I also tend to oversimplify the problems. I wish the Middle East peace.

South America

My first trip to South America was to speak at a conference in Sao Paulo, **Brazil**. It was the first conference I had to use a translator since most of the attendees spoke Portuguese. English is truly the global language and almost all businesspeople around the globe speak it fluently, but my host in Sao Paulo was concerned that the attendees might not all understand it well and wanted the translator. The conference was uneventful, but I was struck by the immense poverty in a shanty town just across the street from my hotel. People were living under pieces of cardboard leaned up against someone else's piece of cardboard. I was amazed years later when I was back in Sao Paulo to see how many of the shanty towns had been razed to make the city look good for the 2016 Summer Olympics. Of course, I could not help but wonder what happened to all the people who lived in them.

I have travelled to most of the South American countries with our South American distributor, Henrik, who is the only guy I know who knows everyone wherever he is. Without exaggeration, we would be walking down the street of some South America city, and people would walk up to us and say, "Hi Henrik," or at least that's what I thought they were saying because they usually were not speaking English.

Rio de Janeiro was spectacular, and staying at a hotel across the street from the world-famous Ipanema Beach made for fun early morning jogs. The Christ the Redeemer Statue is one of the world's most well-known icons, and going to the top of the mountain to stand under it was awe-inspiring. Rio is another electric city with high energy and plenty to do, day or night.

Buenos Aires was another fun city with incredible food, especially the beef with chimichurri sauce and empanadas. The city has a delta that makes for incredible boating, and I was surprised to see thousands of boats on the water the day I spent on the delta. I left **Argentina** sensing that the country had a very bright future.

One of my most emotional travel days was spent in Santiago, **Chile**. When I arrived in Santiago, the country was in suspense and scared for the lives of thirty-three miners who had been trapped underground for nearly ten weeks. It was global news, and my trip unexpectedly coincided with their rescue. The city was jubilant. Cars were flashing their lights and honking their horns, people were dancing in the streets, and everyone was celebrating. It is interesting to see what bliss the release of the miners produced, and though those thirty-three men have had a tough time adjusting since their rescue, as you can easily research, that day, there was great joy.

Colombia, Uruguay, Paraguay, Ecuador, and **Peru** have all also provided fun travel adventures, and like most places, the people of South America always made me feel welcome.

The Caribbean and Central America

James Michener's *Caribbean* is a wonderful historical novel that captures the essence of the islands. Most of the Caribbean islands have a rich history that has been impacted by explorers, the slave trade, and of course, hurricanes.

Living in Florida, I have had an opportunity to visit about twenty of the Caribbean islands either on vacation, service trips, or for work. The islands offer incredible culture and, of course, beautiful beaches and scenery. I'll touch on a few of them below:

Cuba was probably my most interesting visit since I went on a trade mission before travel from the U.S. for tourism was legal. I stayed in a hotel in the heart of Havana, just across the street from the city's Central Park. I was there about four days and was comfortable walking the streets of Havana late at night and peeking in the exciting clubs and restaurants. Other than being approached a couple times by people offering to sell me items or services of which I was not interested, and which I am sure were illegal, I felt perfectly safe. I spent a lot of time during the day outside Havana visiting various marine industry businesses and was most surprised at the lack of Castro shrines, pictures, etc. I expected there would be a lot of Castro propaganda but saw virtually none.

After a few visits to **Haiti**, the poverty in the country does not get any easier to see. It is hard to believe that in the twenty-first century, people must live in those conditions. I have toured schools, churches, and hospitals in Haiti, and while I have enjoyed the food there, it is a very challenging place to live.

Visiting **Aruba**, I was surprised to see that the island is basically a desert, even with cactuses. The desert and tropical contrast made the island interesting, and Aruba has beautiful beaches with enjoyable restaurants and music like many of the islands, so it is a fun place to visit.

St. Maarten, the Netherlands half of an island shared by **St. Martin**, the French half, definitely has the most unique airport. Because the island is small, the runway is up against a public beach, and while I didn't see many locals there, on the beach, tourists have 747s landing just over their heads, literally less than a hundred feet off the ground. It feels like you can reach up and touch them. There are some cool videos on YouTube of planes landing over this beach full of people. I encourage you to check them out.

Central America is a beautiful place that has struggled with revolution, bad government, and other challenges that have kept it from reaching its potential. I've been to all the Central American countries either on vacation or service trips and have always enjoyed my time there. It is important to be aware of safety when visiting Central America; however, other than a night in **Panama** when people were trying to get into my hotel room at 3 a.m., I have generally felt secure in the region.

Costa Rica is a wonderful place to visit on vacation with the rainforests, nice beaches, and great fishing. On one visit, our family was on a river boat cruise and saw HUGE crocodiles in rivers with kids bathing and swimming. Men and women were both fishing in the same rivers with no poles, just string wrapped around their hands. Apparently, they understand the risk the crocodiles present but have learned to live with it out of survival. While we were in Costa Rica, there was a tourist killed by one of the scary reptiles.

Europe

Having been to Europe dozens of times visiting most of the continent's countries, I feel like I should write a separate book just on my travels there. The one thing that always impresses me in Europe is the incredible sense of history a traveler feels when visiting the continent, especially coming from the U.S.

Knowing it will barely scratch the surface of all I have learned in Europe, I will share some of the places that have been most impactful to me.

Normally, I prefer places that are as different as possible, but in London, **England**, the similar language (well, close to similar) makes visiting there simple. There is so much history in London, and the city is easy to get around because of the tube. No need to stay in the prime locations; if the hotel is walking distance to a tube station, it will work. The Tower of London, Westminster Abbey, and Buckingham Palace are popular places to visit, but the city is full of both historic and interesting spots. My most interesting visit to London was just days after Princess Diana died and the city was in mourning. I visited Kensington Palace where the Princess lived, and the flowers were three feet deep surrounding the palace for as far as I could see. I wondered where all the flowers came from and was surprised when the first card I picked up off the flowers was from a group of students at Wynnebrook Elementary School, which is located just a couple miles from the house in West Palm Beach where I was then living. What are the odds of that?

When in London, there are plenty of opportunities to get out of the city. Visits to Shakespeare's home in Stratford-upon-Avon, a nearby castle, Cambridge, Oxford, and of course Stonehenge are all fun day trips from the city. And, for those who have a little more time, visits to Wales and Scotland are spectacular.

My first trip to *Ireland* was with my daughter Erin, who picked the country as a place she would like to visit. We enjoyed walking around Dublin and even visited a village where the residents had built a tower to watch the coast for invading Vikings. When the Vikings would come, the entire village would get inside the tower and close it in a way the Vikings could not open and stay there until the invaders left. Ireland was very expensive when we were there, but I recall our hotel had a free afternoon tea with snacks that Erin and I would go to each day to fill ourselves up.

Visiting Belfast in **Northern Ireland** felt overwhelming when I was there. For much of my life, I had read about the horrible violence in Belfast between Catholics and Protestants, in what most people refer to as "The Troubles." Most of the high wall that separates the Catholic and Protestant sides of the city remains, but today, there are openings that allow people to easily pass through. As I passed from one part of the city to another, I could not help but think that for most of my life, I could have been killed for doing this. Cab drivers and other locals had shared stories of how stressful life was before the peace agreement, with people hating each other and terrorism a constant threat. I couldn't help but feel sad that people had to live that way. On a lighter note, in Belfast, I really enjoyed touring the shipyard that built the Titanic.

Not far from Ireland but a place few go is the *Isle of Man*. In the Irish Sea between England and Ireland, it is best known as a tax haven that hosts the "tt," a motorcycle race around the island. The Isle of Man is spectacular.

Monaco, fully surrounded by *France* and near both the French Riviera and the Italian border, is the second smallest country in the world, the most densely populated, and maybe the richest. It is also one of the most interesting to visit. The casino in Monte Carlo,

Monaco's largest district, is world-renowned, and the parking area in front of it has been filled with extremely expensive European sports cars both times I was there. One of my visits was just a couple days after the Monaco Grand Prix, and our taxi drove the course through the City. Being on the busy streets winding through luxury hotels and condos with the race signage and seating still in place was a fun experience, even though it was a little slower than the race cars a couple days before.

The smallest sovereign country in the world is **Vatican City**, in Rome. Though not Catholic, our family enjoyed our visit to the Vatican despite a little problem getting Erin into St. Peter's Basilica. The Vatican is divided up into three primary parts tourists can visit; the Vatican Museums, the Sistine Chapel, and St. Peter's Basilica. The basilica is considered one of the grandest Christian churches in the world, and tradition states that St. Peter is buried below the altar. The Sistine Chapel was breathtaking, though smaller than I anticipated, and the museums were full of amazing paintings and sculptures. Though not unusual for a European museum, the paintings and sculptures in the Vatican depicted many people without clothing, and we did not think much of it until we walked from the museums to the basilica. It was interesting that after spending time in the Vatican museums with a lot of artistic nudity, security at the basilica would not let Erin in because she was wearing a sleeveless top. She and I laughed about it as we ran to buy her a t-shirt, with sleeves, at one of the many Vatican souvenirs stands in Rome, just off the Vatican property. Apparently, this happens often because the man selling t-shirts looked at Erin and, in English, with a thick Italian accent, said, "So, you have a problem with the church?" We both laughed.

The Baltic countries (**Estonia**, **Lithuania**, and **Latvia**) are full of wonderful people and always a pleasure to visit. Having been under Soviet domination for decades was a challenge for these countries, but the residents are resilient and have done well since the fall of the Soviet Union.

Riga, the capital of Latvia, is a charming town with an old Eastern European feel, and I always enjoy visiting. One night, while having dinner at a wonderful restaurant on the Daugava River that runs through the town, my hosts and I noticed a significant fire not far away but on the other side of the river. The blaze was huge, and it was near my hotel. As we were enjoying our dinner with some concern about what was clearly a significant fire, we realized the fire was burning at Riga Castle. Construction of Riga Castle started in the 1300s, and it had been through several iterations and uses up until its then-use as the presidential palace. The Latvians were heartbroken, and I was sad to see such a beautiful and historic building in flames. I watched well into the night from my hotel. I look forward to seeing the restored castle on my next visit to Latvia.

Like the Baltics, *the Balkans* were under Soviet domination from just after WWII until the collapse of the Soviet Union. Unfortunately, unlike the Baltics, the Balkans post-Cold War transition was not peaceful. The Balkans have a several-century-long history of many ethnic groups generally living together in peace as part of the Ottoman empire and later as part of Yugoslavia. However, the post-Cold-War breakup of Yugoslavia into separate nations unleashed ethic cruelties of disgraceful proportions. I have visited *Slovenia, Croatia, Montenegro,* and *Albania*, beautiful countries bordering the Adriatic Sea, and it is hard to even imagine the horrible cruelty and ethnic cleansing that took place there. Today, except for Albania, those countries are the playground of the rich and famous, and while I am neither rich nor famous, I have enjoyed my time in the Balkans appreciating their beautiful countries and getting to know people there who have lived through a very challenging past.

During high school, my daughter Amanda was very interested in *Greece*, so she and I took a trip there to learn what we could about their fascinating history. After landing in Athens, our trip started out interestingly as I mistakenly hired an unlicensed taxi who dropped us off about three blocks from our hotel. Walking three blocks through Athens at midnight the first time I had visited and not knowing what was around the hotel, especially with my teenage daughter and I towing our suitcases, was not my idea of the best way to start the trip, but fortunately, it ended up being the worst part of the trip.

As an American, the sense of history when visiting Europe is always awe-striking, but Greece is at the top of the historical heap. The Acropolis, including the Parthenon, Hadrian's Library, site of the first Olympic games, the prison of Socrates, and so much more brings history to life in Athens. Standing on Mars Hill, it was easy to imagine the apostle Paul speaking to the leaders of Athens. Athens is a city like no other that provided an environment during the Greek empire for amazing discoveries and the advancement of knowledge. The Athenians were learners; it is interesting to think how history might have progressed if Greece did not fall to the Romans, who were less interested in intellectual challenges, in 146 B.C.

Having grown up in the U.S. during the Cold War, it felt odd flying into Moscow's Sheremetyevo International Airport. After hearing stories of the authoritarian Soviet government that President Reagan called "the evil empire," for most of my life, it felt wrong flying into **Russia** even though the Cold War had ended years before my arrival.

Moscow was more vibrant than I expected, and visiting Red Square, the Kremlin and, of course, St. Basil's Cathedral was exciting. Seeing buildings in town such as the Soviet TASS news agency and the old KGB offices brought back memories of feeling nervous just hearing about the Soviet machine. After reading his book, *Deep Undercover*, I had the opportunity to become friends with ex-KGB agent Jack Barsky, and hearing his stories, in addition to visiting Moscow, really brings the Cold War to life.

Russia is still today a bit of a mystery. I heard about large families living in very small Moscow apartments but also saw tremendous affluence. Much of Russia's private wealth is held by oligarchs who unfairly benefited by acquiring state-owned assets at a small percentage of their actual value. Unfortunately, these privatization programs were overseen by U.S. academics who created a big problem for today's Russia.

One of my favorite European cities and my most pleasant surprise, was Budapest, **Hungary**. Budapest reminded me of Paris but, in some ways, nicer. My hotel on the Danube River was directly across the river from Gellert Hill and the Citadella. I did not have a lot of time in Budapest but did manage to sneak in a tour that showed off the splendidness of the city including a beautiful basilica, synagogue, the Hungarian Parliament, and the famous castle district. I have recommended Budapest to many people over the years and look forward to returning.

Growing up and even as an adult, I've heard my mother say something was as "solid as the Rock of Gibraltar," and it inspired me to check out this Rock for myself. **Gibraltar** is an incredibly strategic spot on the southern tip of the Iberian Peninsula that is the home of not only Gibraltar but also **Spain, Portugal,** and **Andorra**, a small country most people don't even realize exists. Gibraltar is not only known for the "Rock," which is so big that it takes up most of the territory, but also the fact that its main road passes right across the runway at the airport. Of course, like train track crossings, traffic is stopped when a plane is taking off or landing, but it is the only international airport I have visited with a public road running across the runway. Look it up on Google Maps, it's interesting. Oddly enough, because the Rock is so big and takes up much of the territory, the best place in Gibraltar to get a picture of the Rock is at the airport. Finally, when in Gibraltar, I stayed at the Sunborn, a fun cruise ship docked in the harbor and set up as a hotel; I highly recommend it.

Paris, **France** is an amazing city with all the glamour one imagines before visiting. Walking from the Arc de Triomphe down the

Champs-Élysées to the Louvre and then on to Notre Dame is an experience that should be on everyone's bucket list. And, of course, there is the Eiffel tower, visible from most places visitors might be.

Apparently, as I learned, the maître d's of the Eiffel Tower restaurant are a bit picky in who they let in for a meal. On one of Leigh's and my early trips to Paris during the 1990s with our friends Gary and Flora, the four of us decided we would like to eat in the Eiffel Tower restaurant, so Gary and I left the ladies on a bench and we went in to talk to the maître d about a table. We were dressed like tourists in jeans and walking shoes, which apparently, the maître d did not think was appropriate for his restaurant. Though it was mid-afternoon and the place was nearly empty, he would not give us a table. Disappointed, we went out to tell our wives, who after a few minutes, decided to try themselves. Gary and I waited outside just a few minutes before the ladies came out and said they had a table and waved for us to come in with them. The look on the maître d's face was priceless when we walked in after just a few minutes before being denied. In the maître d's defense, I would have let Leigh and Flora in before us guys too.

Any trip to Paris is not complete without a day trip to Versailles where it is hard to imagine people actually lived in such luxury. From my experience, the people in the village outside Versailles much prefer you not speak English, but when they realize that is all you speak and a sale of whatever they are selling is in the balance, they will normally remember they do speak English themselves.

There is so much of Europe that I have not written about, including spectacular places like Rome and Scandinavia that will change you. I love visiting the continent and always learn something there.

North America

Having the opportunity to travel through **Mexico**, much of **Canada**, and all fifty **U.S. states** makes clear the vast amount of diversity in

North America. As I meet and speak to people around the world, it is interesting how many people travel to Disney in Orlando and think they have seen the U.S. There is tremendous diversity in demography and terrain in North America, and you have to spend a lot of time here to get a good feel for the continent.

In Mexico, I have particularly enjoyed spending time in Cancún and Cozumel. While both areas can be touristy, they are still a nearby place to relax and enjoy both the sun and some legitimate Mexican food. Visiting the Mayan ruins in Mexico is fun too, but going in the summer can be blazing hot. Plus, on a visit with my family, it was a little disconcerting when my teenage daughters were continually asked, "Would you like a Mayan boyfriend?" by the locals.

Canada too is a wonderful place to visit. Vancouver, the Canadian Rockies, and the Mont- Tremblant areas are particularly nice and fun to visit.

Finally, I am not even going to try to mention my favorite places in the U.S. There is so much diversity and so many different things to do that a traveler could spend their entire life just traveling and enjoying the U.S. Many do.

Visiting new places will change you as you soak in the terrain, people, and culture. New places, particularly those places outside your comfort zone, can expand your thinking like few other things.

Reflections

- Travel is an important part of being a learner.
- New people, places, and culture expand our thinking in ways we cannot even imagine.

Chapter 8

Musings of a Traveler

Meeting others around the globe provides the traveler a quick realization of how people in diverse cultures view the world differently—and we all believe our way of viewing the world is the "right" way.

For instance, some cultures like the U.S. tend to be more individualist, while others like China are much more collective in their thinking. Some cultures, like Jamaica's, tolerate a lot of uncertainty, while others, like Germany's, try to reduce all uncertainty. Some countries—Thailand, for example—tend to have very cooperative cultures, while most European countries as well as the U.S. are more competitive. Finally, the differences in how people view time is often the most aggravating to people who view it either way. If you are from Switzerland, punctuality is important to you, but if you are from the Caribbean or Latin America, not so much.

Most of us believe our culture is best, but I am certain that if any of us grew up in a different culture, we would embrace it. There is so much we can learn from striving to understand different cultures and perspectives. We really have such a narrow viewpoint on most things and can benefit tremendously from being open to other perspectives. That's why it is so important to be a learner.

For those interested in learning more about cultural differences, David Livermore has written several good books on the topic.

Those who know me best know that I have spent much of my adult life trying to better understand how people are wired and how it impacts both personal and work relationships. I've spent a lot of time studying tools that help with this quest, including Predictive

Index, Myers-Briggs, and DISC. In fact, I was so curious that I earned certifications in both Myers-Briggs and DISC.

What I have learned is that people are wired differently, and understanding that wiring can make you dramatically more effective in both personal and work relationships. After a lifetime of meeting people all over the globe and trying to learn all I can about how we are wired, the following thoughts jump out:

- Very few people are self-aware. When people learn about themselves through reading and using the tools above, it dramatically impacts how they see themselves and improves how they interact with other people.

- The same tools help us understand why others act as they do. It helps take the emotion out of our response regarding the actions of others if we understand that is how they are wired.

- The people who enjoy the best personal and professional relationships embrace the differences between themselves and others. I have learned that when others see things differently, instead of discarding their perspective, I need to understand why.

- Emotion always trumps logic. It's virtually impossible to use logic to argue against someone's emotional position. Wait for the emotion to subside before even trying.

- Constructive debate and conflict are good, even productive. However, constructive conflict and debate is almost impossible without trust.

- Most people are trapped by their own experience and are looking for information to validate what they already think, not to learn.

Overall, it is interesting how similar we all are. If we understand ourselves and others better, we can be so much more effective in all we do. Being both an insatiable reader and global traveler leads to a lot of opportunities to see things differently and learn. Traveling and reading expands thinking in a way that is hard to replicate. It also leads to some thoughts that really don't fit in other chapters. So, here goes.

Where Is the News?

It is fun to read newspapers in foreign countries and watch their news on TV, and there is often an English version of both in major international hotels. Frequently, when there is big news happening around the world, it isn't even mentioned by U.S. news sources. Almost always, there are newsworthy topics being discussed by people I have visited around the world that most Americans know nothing about.

The morning of July 11, 2011, I woke up in Cyprus with no electricity in my hotel. It was frustrating because I was supposed to leave the Mediterranean island that morning and needed electricity in the room to help me prepare for my departure. As I walked through the hotel halls that had emergency lighting on, I could sense something big had happened. After arriving at the front desk, I was told there had been a huge explosion at a local port which, though miles away, had even blown out some windows at my hotel. Later, when driving to the airport, there was residue of the blast on the highway—it was obviously a huge explosion, similar to the Beirut blast that happened later in 2020.

Before leaving Cyprus later that day, I learned that in 2009, the U.S. Navy had seized a Russian ship being used by Iran, full of munitions and bound for Syria, and had asked the government of Cyprus to accept the ship and offload the weapons. The munitions had been offloaded, and because of geopolitical disputes, they were still in Cyprus. A fire the morning I was in Cyprus caused the munitions to explode, resulting in the largest non-nuclear explosion of the twenty-first century (prior to the 2020 Beirut Explosion), which killed thirteen people, injured many more, and created property damage for miles around.

Despite this seeming to be a significant international news event involving the U.S., a Russian ship, Iran, and Syria, I could find nothing about it in the U.S. news. I had experienced global news events not being reported in the U.S., but I had just lived through a big one, and there was no news about it back home. I wondered how often that happens and how informed we really are in the U.S.

I have concluded that in the U.S., it is easy for us to develop positions on issues about which we only know a tiny bit. I understand that only so much news can be reported and the networks have to make money—most of which is made via America's fascination with celebrities—but I have learned that on most issues, we only have a very small amount of information. Being a learner helps us overcome this.

Random Thoughts

In addition to realizing that the average American knows relatively little about world events, we also struggle with more mundane issues like money management and fitness as well as effective education. I want to share a bit about my experiences with these issues.

Money

NYC, Monaco, Palm Springs, Cannes, Palm Beach, Dubai, Hong Kong, and Nantucket are some of the richest places in the world, and they are all fun to visit. Many people can only dream of living in one of those places, and most of those dreaming think there is a connection between wealth and happiness.

Travelling has provided me the opportunity to visit many of the world's richest places, and much of my career was spent working with the world's richest people. If there is one thing I have learned, it is that there is no connection between wealth and happiness. In fact, if there is a connection, it might be a negative correlation.

Anyone researching the topic, or even those of us who know people who have lived through it, knows that lottery winners and people who inherit money end up with significant and unexpected challenges. In particular, unearned wealth seems to create problems for people. The house I currently live in was once owned by a couple who won the lottery, bought the house, and then lost the house when they ran out of money.

The hedonic treadmill is a psychological idea that identifies the tendency for us to never be satisfied, even when we get what we want. Even people who earn a lot of money themselves tend to just want a little bit more. In fact, getting what we want can be a curse because it results in a never-ending cycle of always reaching for something just out of reach. Therefore, the idea of a treadmill that keeps us running but not getting anywhere—anywhere being defined as peace, joy, and contentment.

Many people, no matter what they earn, spend just a bit more than they make, running on the hedonic treadmill. The sad part is that this results in us spending tremendous energy chasing what won't make us happy. Isn't it interesting that what we think will make us happy actually brings more stress and unhappiness into our lives?

My grandfather, Pap, as my cousins and I called him, never made much money, but I remember him telling me more than once, "Son, it's not what you make that matters, it's what you save." Pap was always private with his finances, but when he passed away at 88, we learned that he had practiced what he preached: Pap was a saver, and his life was better for it.

But if money is not happiness, what is? I have learned that the people who are genuinely happy have faith, good relationships, humility, and enjoy serving others. It isn't overly complicated, but coming to that realization can be a long, and sometimes painful, journey.

Doing Different Things

I have always said that if I went back to college for another degree, it would be in psychology. So, it's not unusual for me to pick up a copy of *Psychology Today* magazine to read on an airplane.

Several years ago, I was intrigued by an article in the magazine about two researchers who analyzed the lives of Nobel laureates in chemistry. The researchers compared their distinguished subjects to other equally well-educated and positioned but less decorated scientists in the same fields. They made the comparison to help identify differences that may give an edge to the successful scientists. Their findings were fascinating.

The researchers discovered that almost all the Nobel laureates had a hobby of significance outside their work in chemistry. Correspondingly (and this is what I found extremely interesting), very few of the second-tier scientists had such outside interests.

The researchers went on to point out that many impressive discoveries were made outside the lab while scientists were away from their normal work surroundings. Similarly, in an interesting twist, it claimed that more than a third of the MacArthur Genius Grant recipients acknowledge having built creative worlds in their own mind. They also mention a Yale study that determined children with vivid imaginations learn faster. These are examples of people stepping out of their normal surroundings to achieve really big things.

There is another example that was not mentioned in the magazine article. It is well known that Isaac Newton, arguably the greatest scientist of all time, attributed many of his most significant discoveries to his time off when the European plague had forced the closing of Cambridge University, where Newton worked. Luckily for us, Newton went back to his farm in Lincolnshire to wait it out. While waiting on his farm, he made many amazing discoveries that allow us to enjoy the technology we couldn't imagine living without today.

Learning from History

Thucydides, the Greek many consider to be the father of history, was the first to put forth the idea that the future can be predicted through an understanding of the past. In other words, if we do things that historically generated certain results, we can pretty much be assured those actions will produce the same results in the future.

More than 200 years ago—during the 1800s—this concept of learning from the past was further solidified by the Scottish scientist James Hutton. In his law of Uniformitarianism, Hutton declared that the forces that produce a certain set of results in the past would produce those same results in the future.

Visiting places of historical significance around the world brings to life so many opportunities to learn not only about the past but how people will react in the future. We cannot expect to keep doing the same things over and over and get different results.

Mark Twain is reputed to have said, "The future does not repeat, but it rhymes."

When I was travelling the globe during the 1990s for speaking engagements, one of my most requested presentations was, "What Does the Future Hold? How Today's Global Trends Will Impact Both You and Your Company." People loved hearing about the future, and I loved digging up information to present and still today consider myself a bit of an amateur futurist. I have enjoyed focusing on the future and still do today; I even took a course in Silicon Valley at Singularity University specifically to learn from the world's leaders in global trends. I have learned that the world is going to be much different in ten years, and it's fun to peek ahead to see what it will be like.

Some of the biggest changes coming will be driven by technology. Computational power is growing exponentially and will drive changes in many technologies. Artificial intelligence, quantum computing, nanotechnology, virtual and augmented reality, additive manufacturing, robotics, solarization and electrification, telematics, and 5G technology will all change our world, and soon. These changes will be huge and unavoidable. A big lesson is that countries that try to hold on to the past will pay a big price, but those who are willing to embrace the future and build economies on it will reap huge windfalls.

Geopolitically, the world is going to change just as significantly, and much of that change depends on what the U.S. does in the next few years.

Many in the U.S. believe the country should back off the global leadership role it has held starting with the creation of the Bretton Woods global framework during WWII. Because of this framework, for almost sixty years, the U.S. has provided the world a safe economic system in addition to providing actual security. If the U.S. backs away from this leadership role during a time of significant global transition resulting from technological and demographic changes, it will not only result in re-arming much of the world but also create a huge vacuum that will need to be filled. China would love to fill the vacuum and has done a great job of gaining control of many of the world's rare earth metals that the future economy will need, but it also has an enormous demographic problem and a long history of not being a good neighbor. The U.S. has kept the world together for decades in exchange for control and economic benefits—if the U.S. backs away from its role as part of this deal, all bets are off.

Fitness

In the 1990s, I was getting a little heavier than I wanted to be, so I started exercising, and it became an important part of my lifestyle. I try to exercise every day I possibly can, even when travelling. At one point, I was so focused on exercising that I became a certified personal trainer.

The benefits of exercise are well-documented, but I have learned two things related to it. First, exercise is not an expense of time; it is an investment. If I exercise six hours a week, I feel like I get at least that much time back in productivity. Second, I have learned that no amount of exercise will make up for a bad diet.

A Rich Personal Life

While I've learned a lot about what our society needs to work on, I've also discovered beautiful moments full of wisdom and happiness. Family really is the most important element in a happy life, in my opinion, and I'll illustrate why.

Traveling with My Girls

Much of the time my daughters Erin and Amanda spent growing up was lived outside of the formal classroom setting—we homeschooled, which provided an unusual opportunity for them to travel with me around the globe for service trips, business, my speaking engagements, or just plain fun. This provided them the opportunity to visit dozens of countries by the time they had both graduated from Grace College in Indiana. It was a wonderful learning experience for them and an opportunity for me to spend one-on-one time with each girl and build our relationships.

It was fun in global airports when I would give them the task of getting us from one gate to another when changing planes. This taught them responsibility and how to get around a big airport with signs in another language. They would need that knowledge one day.

For better or worse, travelling with their dad put the travel bug in both my girls. They went with some of their fellow college students on trips to India and Israel while at Grace. Since graduating, Amanda has spent much of her time in Asia, and Erin has travelled there to visit her. They both enjoy and are comfortable travelling globally.

It is very hard to explain the way travel expands the thinking of kids, but seeing other people and cultures helps them see the world in a fuller and better way. Service trips in particular can significantly impact kids in a positive manner. I feel very fortunate that my girls had that opportunity, but there is a downside.

When I was growing up, our family wore the road out between Palm Beach Gardens, Florida, and Oxford, North Carolina. We always went on vacation to the same place: my grandparents' house on Coleman Street in Oxford. It was a small two-bedroom house, and we would sleep on cots in the hall or any other place we could find. However, the memories were grand and irreplaceable.

Summer after summer, and occasionally at Christmas, we would spend time in Oxford enjoying the small town with my grandparents and lots of extended family. We would "take a drive in the country" almost every day and visit any family who might be home. I would occasionally work in my Uncle Wilbur's tobacco warehouse and hang out with Uncle Bernard as he sold fertilizer and pesticides to the farmers. It was especially fun being there when the harvest came in and the auction excitement took place. The auctioneer shouting out things I couldn't understand, the subtle bidding, and moving from one pile of tobacco to another for the next bidding was thrilling to a kid. And, finally, my grandmother's southern cooking, combined with BBQ from our favorite restaurant, made the eating delicious.

Even today, when I am in North Carolina on business, I still try to get to Oxford and visit favorite sites and, of course, my dad who is buried in the local cemetery. It is very hard not to feel emotional when travelling back to this little town and recalling all the memories that were made there.

I am happy that my daughters have been able to see the world, but I am also sorry about what they have missed. They don't have an Oxford in their lives, and I wish they did.

Best Family Vacations

There is not an Oxford in the lives of my daughters, but they did get to visit some cool places. We visited much of the United States and a good part of the world, which resulted in some really fun stuff as a family. Our two most fun vacations, however, took place in the U.S., in confined spaces as a family.

One year, a friend of mine in Arizona loaned our family his sixty-foot houseboat on Lake Mead for a week. Honesty, I panicked when only a few hundred yards from the marina I realized that I would not have cell service for the entire time we were out. It took about a day for the panic to subside, my heart rate to slow, my breathing to settle, and the hives to go away, but we had an amazing week with our family friends, Kevin and Hannah, who we had invited to join us.

Lake Mead is in the desert, so each day, we would move the houseboat from one cove to another before we pulled it bow-first up on the sand, pounded stakes into the ground, and tied the boat up for the night. We grilled our dinners each night and enjoyed our time swimming in the crystal-clear water. I normally like to be on the go and make the use of every vacation minute, but this trip was glorious in its lack of things to do. We could relax, play games, and swim without worrying about anything else.

We enjoyed the houseboat trip so much that we did it again the next summer, this time inviting my mom and my brother Doug's family to join us. Despite a horrendous middle-of-the-night storm that unmoored the houseboat, spun it around, and landed it sideways on the beach, this was a great trip. In retrospect, even the storm was a fun adventure. All six of the kids on that trip still say it is near the top of their favorite vacations.

Our second-favorite family trip was similar, but in an RV. We flew into Rapid City, South Dakota, and spent a week RVing to Mt. Rushmore, The Badlands, Yellowstone, and Grand Teton National Park before wrapping the trip up in Salt Lake City. A week full of buffaloes, national parks, geysers, mountains, monuments, and camping kept our family engaged with the wonder of the Dakotas, Wyoming, Montana, and Utah. I remember reading once in a parenting book that camping is the best family vacation because it always leads to unexpected adventures, which builds the best family memories, and this trip was no exception to that rule.

While driving through Yellowstone, Amanda was in the back of the RV and yelled "stop!" Not sure what was going on, I pulled over to learn the back window of the rented RV was falling out. We caught the window before it fell on the road and smashed, but it was just luck and Amanda's quick shout that kept it from falling out entirely. We stored the window in the RV's restroom and drove for a while without it before finding some Visqueen and duct tape to close the gaping hole in the back of our RV. When we got back to camp, the ranger came to our site and asked what happened before telling us we could not stay in the park anymore. Apparently, he was worried the food in our RV, including us as potential food, would be a bear magnet and the Visqueen was not adequate protection while we were sleeping. We had seen some pretty big grizzly bears in the park, so we were disappointed but didn't need much persuasion to understand the problem. We didn't know where we could go with our bear magnet RV, but fortunately, we found a place outside the park where we felt safe to camp. I learned that before renting an RV, be sure to check out the back window.

On the same trip, we had an oddly related adventure when I was thrown into the glass window we were storing in the bathroom as the RV accelerated, smashing the glass but miraculously leaving me unhurt. We picked up glass from the RV floor and put it all in the bathroom before sealing the bathroom door up with the remaining duct tape we had bought to seal up the missing back window. We wouldn't be using that bathroom anymore, but as I had read in the parenting book, camping makes memories.

It wasn't camping, but a yearly trip to New York City was the closest our family had to an annual vacation trip. We loved going to the Big Apple, and the city was always electric. Staying in Times Square was a great launchpad for a few days of fun each year, and we looked forward to the annual trip.

Investing time with my nephews, Jonathan, Joshua, and Luke, was important, and all three of the boys actually lived with us at various times. When they each were about ten years old, I took them on a trip with just the two of us: Jonathan and I went to Seattle, Joshua and I went to New York City, and Luke and I went to San Francisco. Those three trips were highlights for me, and they seemed to enjoy the time too. We had a lot of exciting times on those trips, but one of the funniest things that happened was with Luke in San Francisco.

I knew Luke was a big fan of Corvette convertibles, so I decided to rent one for our time in California, but I didn't tell him. We landed at the airport, and I was happy that the rental car agency had a bright yellow Corvette convertible for us, but as we walked to get the car, I had still not told Luke. I saw the Corvette as we got closer to it and could tell Luke was getting excited to see it, but he still had no idea it was ours. As we peeked at the Corvette, I sneakily mentioned to Luke that the keys were in it. Finally, I whispered to

Luke "let's take it," and he seemed really surprised, probably wondering what alien had taken over his Uncle Bill. Shortly after we got in the Corvette and drove away with the top down, I told Luke the truth, and he seemed both relieved and happy. It was the start of a fun few days together.

Travelling as a family is a wonderful way to build memories that will last forever, as I was recently reminded when receiving a note from one of my daughters thanking me for the wonderful times we had.

Parenting

When my daughter Erin was born on a Father's Day weekend, I desperately wanted to be a good dad. I had an amazing dad myself who set a great example for me, and I knew if I could be half the dad he was, it would be a home run. So, I did what I normally do when I want to improve: I started reading—and it was a *lot* of reading. I didn't count them, but my guess is that over the years, I've read close to a hundred books about parenting. Besides spending a lot of time with my girls, including travelling with them, reading so many books about parenting helped me learn a lot. I am not saying I was a perfect dad because I clearly wasn't, but I did learn a lot, and I believe, admittedly biasedly, that my daughters grew up to be amazing women. Some of my key learnings as part of my parenting education included:

- Making faith important to our kids helped them understand not only that there is a God that loves them, but also helps them provide context for their world. While, as I wrote in the Faith chapter, there is plenty of evidence to demonstrate the truth of Christianity, we also taught our kids to respect everyone.

- Respecting everyone went well beyond just faith. When Erin was ten years old, we had someone who was looking to buy a house we were selling actually ask if there were any black people on the street. We were appalled, but I was deeply encouraged when Erin asked, "Why would it matter?" It ended up being a teachable moment.

- Speaking of teachable moments, kids learn way more if you teach them when they are open to learning versus when their parent is caught up in the emotion of a moment. The best parents are always on the alert for teachable moments.

- Delayed gratification is one of the most important concepts we can teach kids. There have been interesting studies done on delayed gratification indicating that kids who learn it develop to be much more successful and happy adults. When my kids were young, I had a friend who was an industrial psychologist tell me it is the single most important thing parents should teach kids.

- Tell kids only once to do something before there are consequences to their disobedience. I wonder why parents will say something like, "Why do I have to tell my kids five times to do something?" when the reason seems obvious. They have to tell them five times because the kids know the parents will tell them five times before there are consequences.

- We told our daughters that there would not be negative consequences if they told the truth. Sure, there were times when they used this deal as a "get out of jail card," but the benefits of developing truthful habits is significantly greater than the missed discipline. I have never wondered if my girls were telling the truth.

- At a parenting conference when our girls were young, I heard a speaker say, "Rules without relationship equals rebellion." I believe that and always tried to maintain a close relationship with my girls.

- Alcohol is a vehicle for trouble with teens, and deferring alcohol use keeps kids out of trouble and lowers the risk of them making life-damaging decisions. I told both of my daughters that if they would avoid alcohol until they were 21, I would give them $2,000 cash on their twenty-first birthday. I was happy to pay.

- As girls become teenagers on their way to becoming women, it can be an awkward time for dads. I remember reading several books on this that helped me understand what the girls were going through; one of the best books was *Reviving Ophelia* by Mary Pipher. The bottom line is that dads often pull away during the most critical time of a girl's life, which adds to their daughter's angst and challenges as dads seem to be distancing when they need them most. Dads need to lean in during this time, not pull away.

As every parent knows, there is much more to be a good mom or dad than these few recommendations; however, I have learned from reading and experience that they help.

Reflections

- There are so many things for us to learn.
- The more we learn the more we realize we don't know.

Epilogue

When Everett from Ignite Press and I were originally discussing the *Education of a Traveler* concept, he wanted to understand what my goal was for the book. Everett asked if I was writing the book to make money, and I said no, I would happily donate the profits to charity. He then asked if I was doing it to get speaking engagements, and I replied no, that while I was happy to speak to groups who would enjoy hearing me, I had "been there, done that" and was not writing the book for more speaking engagements.

After a couple more prompts that I answered negatively, he asked directly why I was writing the book.

What I shared on that call with Everett is still my motivation as I wrap up this book. I hope to inspire people to expand their thinking and become "learners." I want to encourage people to be readers and travel. Even one international trip can have a big impact on a person's thinking; if this book can be the catalyst for that trip, I would be happy.

In May of 2019, I was honored to give a commencement address at the University of Central Florida, and there were about 10,000 people at the event. With about 1,000 graduates who needed to walk across the stage and get their well-earned diplomas, I was only allotted about ten minutes for my address, but I wanted it to be impactful. As I considered how to inspire the new graduates and what I could say that could change their life for the better, I decided to speak about being a learner. I knew that was a strange topic to share with people graduating from college, but I also knew that if I could encourage them to become learners, it would impact a lot of lives for the better—and not only the lives but also the people with whom they come in contact. For anyone curious, the commencement address is easily found on YouTube.

Living life as a learner is exhilarating. Reading and travelling are the two best ways I know to become one; if you can do them both, all the better. If sharing the stories in *Education of a Traveler* inspire just a few people to become learners, I will have reached my goal and the world will be better.

Will You Share the Love?

Hey, it's Bill here.

While I hope you found this book interesting, more importantly, I hope it encouraged you to be a learner!

If you enjoyed reading Education of a Traveler, and would be willing to give it a rating wherever you bought the book, it would be appreciated.

Much love and best wishes,

Bill Yeargin

Appendix
100 BOOKS THAT WILL CHANGE YOU

Someone once said that a year from now, we will be the same person we are today except for the places we go and the books we read. St. Augustine said, "The world is a book, and those who do not travel only read one page," while George R.R. Martin added, "A reader lives a thousand lives before he dies. The man who never reads lives only one."

As a young kid, maybe eight or nine, I remember being excited on Saturday mornings when the Bookmobile would come into our neighborhood. I would run up to the Little General convenience store where it was parked for the morning and return the previous week's book I had borrowed before searching through the big bus for a new book. I guess I was a nerd.

As the decades passed, my passion for reading continued to grow, and even now, I finish dozens of books each year. I always have two books going, one on my Kindle and one on my Audible app. Though it's now old-fashioned, occasionally I will even read the hard copy of a book.

Reading to learn new things is exciting. Sometimes, people are surprised to hear about my reading choices, but I much prefer to read something that challenges my thinking rather than something that validates it. Learning is a great feeling, and few things are as exhilarating as having my mind changed or seeing things from a new perspective.

It is hard for any prolific reader to select just a few books to recommend. However, any story of this traveler's education would not be complete without referring to some of the books that I have found impactful, even if it feels like I am just scratching the surface of what I should share. Since you have made it this far in *Education of a Traveler,* you likely enjoy reading too. So, if you haven't read them, I will share some books that have impacted me, in no particular order.

Non-Fiction

For many years I would only read non-fiction and still enjoy great non-fiction books today. Some of the books that have impacted my thinking include the following.

The Meritocracy Trap by Daniel Markovits shares how a concept that is accepted by almost all Americans, reward based on merit, often has the opposite of its desired effect.

Harvard professor David Sinclair's book, **Lifespan**, shares new thinking on aging and how we can dramatically slow its effects.

The Nature Fix by Florence Williams investigates the science of how the environment impacts our mood, health, and creativity. She demonstrates that we are much better people when we invest time in nature.

My good friend Wallace "J" Nichols wrote **Blue Mind** about the power of water on our lives. "J" uses science to motivate his readers to get as much time as possible on, in, near, or under the water.

The classic **Man's Search for Meaning** was written by Victor Frankl after a long stay in German concentration camps where his wife and parents were killed. Frankl explains that almost everything can be taken from us except the freedom to choose our attitude regarding our circumstances.

In the classic **The Sunflower**, by Simon Wiesenthal, the author also writes about his time in a German concentration camp, including his refusal to forgive a dying German guard who asked for his forgiveness. Decades later, Wiesenthal wrestles with his decision in the book that also includes advice to him from many of the world's leading philosophers and theologians.

The Great Influenza by John Barry tells the story of the 1918–19 Spanish flu, which would have been more appropriately named the Kansas flu, and by some accounts, it killed nearly a hundred million people. The parallels between the Spanish flu and COVID-19 are interesting.

The Coddling of the American Mind by Lukianoff and Haidt demonstrates how we are setting a generation up for failure by limiting their thinking to what makes them feel good.

Travels with Lizbeth by Lars Eighner is the true story of a gay writer who lost his job and ended up homeless for three years, sleeping on the streets with his dog Lizbeth.

13 Days is a memoir of the Cuban Missile Crisis written by JFK's confidant and brother, Robert F. Kennedy.

Barbara Tuchman wrote the classic **The Guns of August** about how WWI started in August of 1914. This fascinating book should be required reading for the leader of every country.

You Are the Placebo by Joe Dispenza shares the science behind the placebo effect and how we can use our minds to keep us healthier.

Michael Grunwald wrote **The Swamp**, an impactful history of the Florida Everglades that taught this native Floridian a lot about his state.

We hear a lot about inequality in our society. In **The Great Leveler**, Walter Scheidel looks back at history and how inequality has ended in past societies, and it's not good. This book will encourage the richest people to ensure they are helping those less fortunate.

The **Same Kind of Different as Me** by Ron Hall and Denver Moore is the touching story of an international art dealer who befriends a homeless man and how their relationship changed both of their lives.

Better Angels of our Nature, written by Harvard professor Steven Pinker, is a fascinating and encouraging book that uses data to demonstrate that we are living in the most peaceful and safe time in world history.

Chuck Collins explains how privilege and entitlement makes those who were **Born on Third Base** think they hit a triple.

Before he became president, John F. Kennedy wrote **A Nation of Immigrants**, which documents how immigration has provided the fuel that has driven the U.S. and created much of the country's success. This book is an interesting read, especially at a time when immigration is a hotly debated subject.

Walter Isaacson, who wrote the Steve Jobs biography, did an outstanding job on the biography **Leonardo DaVinci**. It is hard enough to be best in the world at one thing, but DaVinci excelled in several disciplines.

Educated by Tara Westover is a must-read. Westover grew up in a cult family who would not let her go to school, but she ended up getting her PhD. A compelling story.

Beth Macy's book **Dopesick** explains just how addicted America is to opioids and the devastating impact it is having on our country.

Timothy Ferriss in his interesting book, **A Tribe of Mentors**, asks successful people from all walks of life what they do to be successful. One interesting takeaway for me was how many of them meditate.

Emotional Intelligence by Daniel Goleman was groundbreaking. Goleman demonstrated that it is not just IQ that determines success but also how we manage our emotions, including self-awareness and empathy. Goleman showed that while we cannot change our IQ, we can improve our emotional intelligence.

Anyone interested in the public education system should read *The Prize* by Dale Russakoff. The story of what happened when Facebook's Mark Zuckerberg donated one hundred million dollars to Newark's public schools is fascinating.

In *The People vs. Democracy*, Yascha Mounk explains why populist candidates may make us feel good but can also be very dangerous to the future of democracy.

A Generation of Sociopaths by Bruce Gibney is an excellent book that demonstrates how Baby Boomers have consistently made decisions that benefitted themselves while leaving the tab for their kids and grandkids to pay.

Race and the Black Experience

Three to four years before the George Floyd incident awakened America to racial inequities, I started on a journey to learn about the black experience in the U.S. The journey started when my daughter, Amanda, recommended I read *Between the World and Me*, written by Ta-Nehisi Coates. The book is a letter to the author's teenage son about what he can expect as a black man in the United States. After reading *Between the World and Me,* I wanted to understand more about the black experience, which started me reading several books that have impacted my thinking on this topic.

Richard Rothstein, in his book *The Color of Law*, provides a succinct description of how segregation has been promoted by the U.S. government over the past two hundred-plus years. This book was an eye-opener for me.

In **The New Jim Crow**, Michelle Alexander describes how America's War on Drugs has been fought largely in black neighborhoods and has resulted in a disproportionate percentage of black men in jail. The authorities focus on black neighborhoods even though all the data indicates that drugs are just as proliferate in white communities as black.

Theologian Drew Hart wrote **Trouble I've Seen** about racism in the church community and what Christians should do.

Robin DiAngelo wrote **White Fragility** about why white people struggle acknowledging racism and why being "color blind" does not help.

Begin Again by Princeton Professor Eddie Glaude uses the life and experiences of famed black novelist James Baldwin to help his readers more deeply understand the black perspective.

The Bluest Eye by Toni Morrison is a classic story about a little black girl who dreams about having blue eyes because she associates them with whiteness.

Some other novels that helped me better understand the black experience were **Dear Martin** by Nic Stone, **An American Marriage** by Tayari Jones, **Sing Unburied Sing** and **Salvage the Bones** by Jesmyn Ward, and the classic **Invisible Man** by Ralph Ellison.

Self-Improvement

As part of my desire to learn and improve, my reading list has included many self-improvement books over the years. A few that stand out are below.

Dr. Maxwell Maltz wrote **Psycho Cybernetics**, a book I read in college that changed my life. While there is plenty to criticize in Dr. Maltz's book, it helped me understand the power of mindset, which has been a big driver for whatever success I have had. A similar and more recent book is **Mind Gym** by sports psychologist Gary Mack. In my opinion, there is no question that how we think impacts both our happiness and the degree of success we experience.

The Seven Habits of Highly Effective People by Stephen R. Covey is the undisputed self-improvement champion that has sold tens of millions of copies. Anyone who has not read this book should drop everything and buy it today. It will change your life for the better.

Another classic is **How to Win Friends and Influence People** by Dale Carnegie. If you want to really learn from this book, sign up for the related Dale Carnegie course; I have taken it and encouraged dozens of my co-workers to take it over the years.

The Purpose-Driven Life by Pastor Rick Warren takes its readers on a forty-day journey to help them find their purpose in life. Spoiler alert—it's not about you!

Leadership and Self-Deception by The Arbinger Institute helps us understand that often, the person we deceive most in life is ourselves.

In Kathryn Schultz's very powerful book, **Being Wrong**, she explains how we can often be a hundred percent wrong while feeling a hundred percent right. Anyone who wants to be a critical thinker needs to read this book.

In the book **Mindset**, Carol Dweck explains that we all have either a fixed or growth mindset. She also explains how life can be so much better with a growth mindset. This is a book that will change how you view the world.

When successful leaders lose everything, the root of their problem is almost always pride. Tim Irwin does a great job of demonstrating this in his book, **Derailed.**

I had the opportunity to meet Dan Buettner and hear him talk about his research for *National Geographic* on places where people live the longest. Buetner shares his lessons learned in the very interesting book **The Blue Zones Solution.**

Ten Percent Happier is ABC News Anchor Dan Harris's story about how meditation changed his life. I frequently use the Ten Percent Happier app when meditating.

Clayton Christenson, the late Harvard professor who was the world's leading thinker on innovation, writes about Harvard students reaching all their professional goals and still feeling miserable in **How Will You Measure Your Life?** This book will make you think about what is important.

In **Learned Optimism**, Martin Seligman uses his decades of clinical research to demonstrate that being an optimist makes life better, much better. I am wired to be an optimist anyway, but this book still had a big impact on my thinking.

Spencer Johnson's **Who Moved My Cheese?** is a simple but powerful classic. Anyone dealing with tough changes should read this book.

Flatland, a novella written in Victorian England by Edward Abbot, is an interesting look at how we can all be captured by our own perspective.

Faith

Every year I try to either read or listen through **The Bible**. If you are doing it for the first time, don't start at the beginning. Start with the New Testament, in the book of Matthew. Just five chapters into Matthew is the Sermon on the Mount, the most famous sermon ever, where Jesus started to change everything.

Other faith books that have impacted my thinking are the following.

Andy Stanley's book **Irresistible** is one of the reasons I recommend you start in the New Testament the first time you read through the Bible. This book both shifted and crystalized my thinking.

My good friend Brant Hansen is a nationally syndicated radio personality and a great author. Brant has spoken to our Correct Craft team several times, and I have given away hundreds of his books; everyone always loves what he has to say and write. If you want great thinking written in an easy-to-read, funny manner, read Brant's books. I would recommend them in the order he wrote them: **Unoffendable, Blessed Are the Misfits,** and **The Truth About Us**.

Eric Metaxas is an outstanding author and has written three Christian biographies that are all compelling reads. **Bonhoeffer**, **Martin Luther**, and **Amazing Grace** (about William Wilberforce) are each outstanding books that will shed tremendous light on their subjects.

Speaking of Bonhoeffer, his book **The Cost of Discipleship** is very good.

Misreading Scripture Through Western Eyes, by Richards and O'Brien explains how we can often misinterpret stories in the Bible because we are viewing them through our Western perspective and culture.

In **Tried by Fire**, William Bennett describes the early church history in a very informative and interesting manner.

Any C.S. Lewis book is good, but I have particularly enjoyed **Mere Christianity** and **The Screwtape Letters**.

After my dad passed away and I was digging deep into my faith, **Evidence That Demands a Verdict** by Josh McDowell helped me solidify what I believe.

Along the same vein, **The Case for Christ** by Lee Strobel is excellent.

In his classic, **The Pursuit of God**, A.W. Tozer explains why we should pursue God and how to do it.

Max Lucado, in **Anxious for Nothing**, explains God's antidote for worry and anxiety.

The Jesus I Never Knew by Philip Yancey helps explain who Jesus was as a person and how He fit into the culture of his time.

Quarantine by Jim Crace is not for everyone. In this novel, Crace tries to share a story of Jesus during His forty days in the wilderness. While there were many things in the book that caused me tension as a Christian, Quarantine also describes what the wilderness would have been like when Jesus was there.

Letters From a Skeptic by Gregory Boyd and his father Ed are a series of letters between the two while the father was skeptical about Christianity. The son addresses his father's very difficult questions and, spoiler alert, the father becomes a Christian.

In his book, **Goliath Must Fall**, Louie Giglio shares how we can overcome the giants in our lives.

Costly Grace, by Rob Schenck, documents his story converting from Judaism to Christianity, becoming a national leader of right-wing politics, and leaving politics to pursue what he calls the purity of the gospel.

Randy Alcorn's book **Heaven** was very beneficial to me as I thought about my dad and his death. Alcorn emphasized how much better heaven will be than we can even imagine.

In **Stranger at the Gate**, Mel White tells his story of being a ghost-writer for and friend of Billy Graham, Jerry Falwell, and Pat Robertson before coming out as gay after many years of marriage and a family. This book broadened my understanding of the challenges gay Christians face.

Fiction

There was a time when I saw little to no value in reading fiction. I wanted to learn and did not see how fiction would help. I have grown to see fiction much differently, as it now provides me an opportunity to both learn a lot and broaden my perspective. The following are some fiction books I have found interesting and/or impactful.

I love historical fiction, and one of the best books I have read in this genre is **Before We Were Yours** by Lisa Wingate. In this novel, Wingate tells the story of an actual true organization, The Tennessee Children's Home, which kidnapped children and sold them to parents looking for adoptions.

James Michener also wrote great historical fiction. All the Michener books I have read are great, but my favorites were **Alaska**, **Hawaii**, **Caribbean**, and my most recent Michener read, **The Source**.

A Land Remembered by Patrick Smith is an outstanding historical novel about Florida. All Floridians should read this book, which will open their eyes regarding what Florida was like before its development started.

Medieval Woman by Ann Baer, is the story of Marion and her medieval family. It is a great work of historical fiction that will make the reader very happy to be alive today.

The Old Man and the Sea and **A Farewell to Arms** are a couple Hemingway novels I have really enjoyed. Hemingway is an icon for his writing, and these books help the reader understand why.

Gulliver's Travels by Jonathan Swift is not only a fun read but also full of lessons on how people view the world differently.

Moby Dick by Melville and *Lord of the Flies* by Golding are a couple other classics I enjoyed with lots of lessons.

Ernest Kline's excellent *Ready Player One* is a relatively new novel but has already become a sci-fi classic in which he describes a dystopian future where many people live through virtual reality.

Graeme Simsion wrote a hilarious series of books about a very quirky genetics professor who is looking for a wife. *The Rosie Project*, *The Rosie Effect* and *The Rosie Result* all had me laughing out loud as I read them.

The Poisonwood Bible by Barbara Kingsolver is a very interesting story of a missionary family in the 1960s Congo and the challenges they face.

Lisa See, author of *The Shanghai Girls*, does a great job telling the story of two sisters who leave war-torn Shanghai for arranged marriages in the United States.

Fields of Fire, written by Reagan Administration Navy Secretary James Webb, is a compelling novel about what it was like to be a marine on the ground during combat in Vietnam.

Margaret Atwood's dystopian novel, *The Handmaid's Tale*, is an interesting story set in New England after the U.S. has been taken over by the tyrannical state Gilead, which oppresses women.

The Uncommon Reader by Alan Bennett is a short and fun novel about the Queen of England becoming an obsessive reader.

Delia Owens' recent novel, *Where the Crawdads Sing*, is a compelling page-turner about a girl growing in the marsh of North Carolina.

The Great Courses

I cannot conclude this section without making a plug for The Great Courses. The Great Courses are lectures by some of the world's most renowned professors on various subjects. I always learn a tremendous amount listening to these courses, and they cover pretty much any topic you want to learn about.

I have been listening to The Great Courses for many years and have finished dozens of their courses. As an example of what they offer, the last four years I have listened to the following courses:

- Socrates, Plato, and the Dialogues
- Your Deceptive Mind
- The Holy Land Revealed
- The Era of the Crusades
- Rise and Fall of the Roman Empire
- Law School for Everyone
- Behavioral Economics
- Native Peoples of North America
- Practicing Mindfulness
- Cognitive Behavioral Theory
- From Yao to Mao
- American Religious History

It's hard to end this section after writing about only a small percentage of the books that have impacted me; honestly, the above list feels totally inadequate, and I have not included many of my favorites. Asking about my favorite books is like asking me which of my daughters is my favorite; I love them both very much and equally. There are so many more books that have been part of my education, but hopefully, the list above will provide some good reading options to either start or continue being a learner. I am thankful to be a reader!

Reflections

- Reading is an important part of being a "learner."
- Reading can expand your thinking exponentially.
- Readers should read to expand, not validate, their thinking.

About the Author

Bill Yeargin is the CEO of Correct Craft. Under Bill's leadership, Correct Craft has won all their industry's major awards and developed a unique culture of "Making Life Better." A passionate lifelong learner, Bill earned an MBA and completed post-graduate education at Harvard, Stanford, Villanova, and MIT.

Having served both the Obama and Trump administrations on cabinet-level advisory councils, *Florida Trend* magazine recognized Bill as one of "Florida's Most Influential Business Leaders."

Bill has been published hundreds of times, has authored four books, and is a sought-after conference speaker.

He and his wife Leigh have two daughters, Erin (married to Ben) and Amanda.

Made in the USA
Coppell, TX
10 September 2021

62122945R00083